Understanding and Teaching Children with Autism

RITA JORDAN AND STUART POWELL

JOHN WILEY & SONS
Chichester · New York · Brisbane · Toronto · Singapore

Copyright © 1995 by John Wiley & Sons Ltd,
Baffins Lane, Chichester,
West Sussex PO19 1UD, England

National (01243) 779777
International (+44) 1243 779777

Reprinted September 1995, January 1996

Other Wiley Editorial Offices

John Wiley & Sons, Inc., 605 Third Avenue,
New York, NY 10158-0012, USA

Jacaranda Wiley Ltd, 33 Park Road, Milton,
Queensland 4064, Australia

John Wiley & Sons (Canada) Ltd, 22 Worcester Road,
Rexdale, Ontario M9W 1L1, Canada

John Wiley & Sons (SEA) Pte Ltd, 37 Jalan Pemimpin #05-04,
Block B, Union Industrial Building, Singapore 2057

Library of Congress Cataloging-in-Publication Data

Jordan, Rita.
    Understanding and teaching children with autism / Rita Jordan and
Stuart Powell.
        p.   cm.
    Includes bibliographical references and index.
    ISBN 0-471-95888-3 (cased) — ISBN 0-471-95714-3 (paper)
    1. Autistic children—Education.   2. Autism.   I. Powell, Stuart.
II. Title.
LC4717.J67   1995
371.94—dc20   95-3852
                                                                  CIP

British Library Cataloguing in Publication Data

A catalogue record for this book is available from the British Library

ISBN 0-471-95888-3 (cased)
ISBN 0-471-95714-3 (paper)

Typeset in 10/12pt Plantin by Vision Typesetting, Manchester
Printed and bound in Great Britain by
Biddles Ltd, Guildford and King's Lynn

Contents

About the Authors

RITA JORDAN combines early experience as a teacher in nursery and primary education with postgraduate degrees in Child Development and linguistics. She was involved in the development of services for preschool children before specialising in the needs of children with learning difficulties, and was for several years deputy principal of a school for children with autism. Rita moved into Special Needs teacher education and teaching clinical linguistics at the University of Hertfordshire, before becoming Lecturer in Autism at the University of Birmingham School of Education, responsible also for distance and campus-based courses for professionals working in the field of autism. She is co-director with Stuart Powell of the Education Research into Autism Group.

STUART POWELL was a teacher and headmaster of two primary schools before becoming lecturer in educational psychology and special educational needs at the University of Hertfordshire. His PhD is in Psychology of Education, and he is now Reader in Educational Psychology, and University Research Tutor, at the University of Hertfordshire, where he combines responsibility for professional development courses in special education, with research in psychology and education of children with autism, and runs the Centre for Autism Studies. He is co-director of the Education Research into Autism Group.

Preface

This book aims to help all those concerned with the education and welfare of children with autism to understand their charges better and thereby to provide more effectively for their education. We talk about 'children' but we accept that autism is a lifelong condition that will require special care and consideration into adulthood. Some of the suggestions in this book, then, will be applicable across the age range even though our focus is clearly on children. Early intervention is advantageous but it is never too late to improve quality of life through greater understanding of individuals with autism and more effective ways of meeting their needs.

We are not claiming to offer a 'miracle cure' for autism but there is evidence to suggest that education can be effective, not only in ameliorating the symptoms of autism, but in tackling some of the fundamental learning difficulties involved. This book, then, offers hope but makes no false promises. Although this is a very exciting time for research into autism, in terms of understanding both its biology and its psychology, at the time of writing there is no known cure. It is important then to be clear about the sense in which one can 'accept' this situation. We think that those working with individuals with autism need to respect the way in which such individuals think and learn. But at the same time it is possible to want to work within the context of the autism to make that thinking and learning more effective.

Autism involves distinctive ways of thinking about the world which lead to particular ways of behaving. Temple Grandin is a very able individual with autism who is very successful as an academic, as a professional designer, and as a business woman; she leads a full life and lectures at conferences around the world.[10] Yet she is still very much aware of thinking and perceiving in a different way to others and says she is glad to be 'autistic' because of the strengths as well as the limitations it brings. Most parents and professionals will find it hard to accept this entirely, and indeed for the majority of individuals with autism additional learning difficulties will make the 'strengths' of autism less evident and the limitations difficult to overcome. Nevertheless, professionals and parents need to understand those ways of thinking and learning as best they can; they need to work within the context of the autism and work with the autism itself.

It should be noted here that we can only describe autism from our own non-autistic perspective. We tend to interpret in terms of what it would be like *for us* to be without certain understandings (e.g. the lack of an ability to understand the intentions of others). This is necessarily a limited perspective and remains so in that we cannot experience from the inside how the world appears to the individual with autism. The closest we can get, perhaps, is by listening to the description of those like Temple Grandin who can tell us something of what it is like to be autistic. But even here there is a limitation in that such individuals are exceptional and in any case they learn to use terms in such a way as to make it easier for the non-autistic to understand.

We nevertheless believe that effective education must be based on the understandings that we do have and not on following some prescriptive 'recipe' approach. We cannot say 'Do this and all will be well', but we can show how to make sense of what the child with autism does and how to build a teaching approach based on this understanding. When we talk about children with autism it is important to recognise that there will be a range of individual differences across a range of dimensions. No two children with autism will think or behave in the same way. In short, each child is very much an individual, and will respond to the autism in his/her own way. Nevertheless, there is enough known about the general ways of thinking in autism to allow some generalisations to be made and this book is based on notions of ways of responding to a particular [autistic] kind of thinking and learning.

In coming to the ideas that are presented in this book we have taken on board the work of people such as Simon Baron-Cohen[2] and Uta Frith[3] and their important and far reaching 'discovery' that individuals with autism have particular difficulty in understanding mental states—their own or those of others. It is not just that they do not understand *what* others are thinking and feeling (which is apparent as lack of empathy) but that they do not even understand *that* they themselves, or others, are thinking and feeling at all. This is an important finding in that it helps to make sense of the thread that runs through much of the pattern of autistic thinking, as will be apparent in later chapters. We should stress that we are not claiming that individuals with autism do *not* think or feel, but that they may not be aware of themselves (or others) doing so.

Perhaps it is important to note here that the most fundamental difficulty arising from this 'deficit' is that people in general become unpredictable. Those of us who are not autistic base our understanding of others and what they are likely to do, not so much on what they have done before, which only works for very limited and structured situations, but on what we *think* they are feeling, wanting and believing. It is very much a matter of us continually interpreting the intentions of others, and it is this process which is at the heart of social interactions and which enables us to function more or less successfully within ever changing social environments. Variation in success for an individual relates substantially to familiarity with social context. One only has to think of how difficult it can be in an unfamiliar social milieu to recognise the social signals, let alone make appropriate responses. Again, to use our non-autistic perspective to interpret the nature of the autistic 'problem', it seems likely that without social understanding, people would appear to be behaving unpredictably and that this would make social contexts and the people within them confusing, possibly stressful, and even frightening. We begin, then, to come closer to an explanation for the social difficulties in autism and it is also possible to see how the theories mentioned above provide more specific predictions of the kinds of difficulties to be found in communication and some of the features of rigidity in thinking and behaviour.

However, even the original research by Baron-Cohen and others showed that a proportion of individuals with autism are able to pass what have been called 'theory of mind' tests, demonstrating some understanding of mental states.[2] Yet the actual behaviour of such individuals in social situations is still 'autistic' and their generally more effective functioning might be attributable to their higher level of intelligence (for it is usually the more able individuals with autism who pass such tests) rather than their performance on 'theory of mind' tasks. Also, the tests that are used tap into a high level of understanding about mental states demonstrated by understanding of false beliefs and this level of understanding is not apparent in normally developing children until four years of age. Clearly, children with autism develop very differently from normally developing children up to the age of four years so the differences cannot reside fully in a lack of a 'theory of mind'. It may be, as the authors of such theories propose, that the difficulties lie in precursors to the theory of mind but then their theoretical account becomes more like that of others who place the fundamental difficulty as occurring much earlier in development.

The significant 'other' here is Peter Hobson who, while not arguing with the research findings in developmental psychology on 'theory of mind' difficulties in autism, reinterprets those findings in the light of his view that autism is a disturbance in intersubjectivity.[11] While this may seem to be a simple reworking of the accepted core deficits in autism, in fact, Hobson locates that disturbance as being at a level of affective relatedness to the world, leading not only to problems in direct social perception but also to problems in categorising and relating to the world in relation to the self. Here there are clear connections with what Frith has identified as a failure to search for coherence and with the notion that we develop in this book that there is, in autism, a failure to develop satisfactorily an 'experiencing self'. In essence, Hobson pushes the explanation of the source of the difficulty in autism beyond the perceptual to the experiential, stressing the importance of what he terms 'perceptually-anchored intersubjective communication'.

We are influenced in our own thoughts by his notion that a kind of affective co-ordination is critical for the sort of interpersonal engagement that is, in turn, so critical for social and intellectual development.

In this book we will argue for the importance of teachers understanding the nature of autism at the psychological level rather than just treating it at a behavioural level. It seems to us that the teacher needs to pay attention to the full range of developmental sequelae that follow from the deficit suggested by Hobson[11] and to develop teaching approaches and curricular content that address each of these areas. But the aim of such approaches should not be limited to teaching normal development in the form of an early developmental curriculum, since there is no reason to suppose that the child with autism is able to benefit from such an approach, beyond the mechanical rote learning of skills, which will be unrelated to understanding and therefore difficult to generalise or extend.

Rather, our interpretation of the pedagogy that follows from the ideas that we have put forward in this preface is that teachers of individuals with autism need to remain aware of all the areas of normal development that the child with autism will be unable to access via the normal affective, spontaneous, intuitional route and to use the route to which they *do* have access (i.e. the general cognitive route) to provide explicit teaching in those areas. The central thesis of this book is that when teaching pupils with autism one needs to recognise the real nature of the problem, since it affects understandings that are so much part of our non-autistic biological endowment that we are seldom aware of them as 'achievements' in any sense. This book will help the teacher to identify these teaching goals, and to develop ways of teaching them explicitly. It also recognises that many children with autism, especially those with additional learning difficulties, will not reach these levels of understanding, even with explicit and direct teaching. It will suggest compensatory strategies that can be taught to help the child move forward in his or her development in spite of those problems and to gain access to as full and meaningful a curriculum as possible.

We also suggest ways in which the environment can be structured to enable learning to occur in spite of the difficulties and to enhance the quality of life for the children both now and in the future. Learning to participate in a society that is to a large extent 'alien' to them is bound to be difficult and there are ethical issues about the degree to which education should insist on conformity. Teachers need to confront these issues and to ensure that what is taught is of benefit to the individual and not just to the particular situation (classroom, school, education system) in which the individual is placed. This book is about helping children to claim their rights to be treated with dignity as well as about meeting their special needs as we have defined them.

We would like to acknowledge our debt to the many staff, parents and children with autism with whom we have worked over the years. We cannot acknowledge them all individually but we would like to make special mention of the staff and pupils of Radlett Lodge School where we have both worked for considerable periods. The book concerns our own interpretations and is largely based on our experiences but we owe much to the special expertise and inspiration of many colleagues and must make mention here of Wendy Brown, Margaret Golding and Katie Thomas.

Introduction

THE AUTISTIC CONTINUUM AND SPECIAL EDUCATIONAL NEEDS

DIAGNOSTIC CRITERIA

In the early days of the general understanding of autism, there appeared lists of 'points' for the diagnosis of the condition, although it was often called 'childhood schizophrenia' at this stage. Sometimes these 'points' (referring to aspects of abnormal behaviour or development) were merely seen as descriptive, i.e. 'salient features', and so there was no clear prescription of which features had to be present in order to make the diagnosis of autism and which were merely features that frequently accompanied autism but were not essential criteria. Apart from misgivings about the nature of some of these points themselves, this also led to the confusing and unacceptable situation whereby two children might be diagnosed as autistic and yet not have a single 'defining feature' in common.

THE TRIAD OF IMPAIRMENTS

There are difficulties in defining autism as a syndrome, because of other developmental problems that often accompany it. Kanner had originally supposed that all children with autism were fundamentally intelligent and that apparent delays in development were a direct result of the autistic condition.[17] Sadly, this is one of the 'facts' about autism that Kanner got wrong and autistic individuals like 'Rainman' (the character in a well-known film) are very rare indeed, even within the population with autism. The majority of individuals with autism have additional learning difficulties, many of them severe. In fact, the more severe the general learning difficulties the more likely the individual is to have autism, although it becomes increasingly difficult to separate out the effects of autism from the effects of severe retardation.

Lorna Wing and Judy Gould, however, found that, even within populations with developmental difficulties, there were a cluster of features that provided diagnostic criteria for autism.[35] These are commonly referred to as Wing's Triad of Impairments in Autism:[34]

1 *Social.* Impaired, deviant and extremely delayed social development—especially interpersonal development.

This is on a continuum from those who might be regarded as classically autistic in that they are solitary and withdrawn, through those who will respond in a passive way when approached by others but will not initiate interaction, to those who appear 'active but odd' in that they seek attention but do not know how to deal with it. A child may begin at one end of this continuum as a classically withdrawn toddler and, through the course of development or through positive teaching, end as an 'active but odd' teenager.

2 *Language and Communication.* Impaired and deviant language and communication—verbal and non-verbal.

The range of spoken language difficulties associated with autism is wide. Again, there are extreme cases, where there are additional language and/or severe learning difficulties, where spoken language never develops. At the other extreme are children who have highly developed language skills in the sense that their grammar and pronunciation are excellent and they may have a special talent for learning foreign languages. Yet, regardless of the level of spoken language competence, there will be problems with all aspects of communication. There will be difficulties in understanding and using facial expressions, expressive gestures, body postures and positionings and (where there is spoken language) some problems with the meaning (semantic aspects) and pragmatic aspects of language. Pragmatics relates to the social understanding and use of language and so it is communication rather than language itself that is affected in autism.

3 *Thought and Behaviour.* Rigidity of thought and behaviour and impoverished imagination.

Autism is characterised by ritualistic behaviour, reliance on routines, and extreme delay or absence of 'pretend play'. As with so much in autism it is not so much that the child with autism cannot play in this way as that such play does not develop spontaneously and, when it is taught, it remains limited to the kinds of play that have been demonstrated; there is little or no creativity. Again, the more able individual with autism may display imagination, but it is also likely to be of a limited kind and there may be difficulty then in distinguishing imagination from reality. It is as if there is no basis for distinguishing mental images from images produced from perception of the environment.

For a diagnosis of autism to be justified then all of these behaviours should be out of keeping with the child's mental age. Most people would also want to limit the diagnosis to conditions with an onset before 30 months of age, although Lorna Wing herself feels there may be cases of late onset autism and this should be included in a broad view of the diagnosis of autism.

This triad of impairments form the basis of the diagnostic criteria used by the World Health Organisation (ICD–10)[36] and the American Psychiatric Association (DSM–IV).[1]

THE CAUSES OF AUTISM

There is no space here to detail the exciting research that is currently underway into the causes of autism, but it is important to discuss the level at which one might talk about causes. And it is important to be clear that because there is not one single identifiable cause, nor ever likely to be so, this does not mean that there is no actual condition with which we can deal. Autism is more than a label attached to a range of symptoms—it is a diagnosis that helps to make sense of the defining features and explain why they co-occur. In order to form a syndrome, the defining features need to be pathological, or deviant from normal development, and reflect some underlying common cause, or at least a common pathway.

Thus, at the level of biology (just as with conditions like cerebral palsy) there may be a number of different 'causes' that lead to this particular dysfunction in the brain. We know that genetic factors play a part but are not the complete answer. There is work showing brain chemical abnormalities that may result from an inborn failure in enzyme production. Certain illnesses in the mother may have damaged the developing foetus or there may have been anoxia or damage at birth. The point is that all these different causes may have a common effect at the psychological level—resulting in the same psychological (in the sense of the functioning of the brain) deficit that defines autism. That in turn will lead to a range of behavioural symptoms that are linked by their dependence on that damaged psychological process.

We can see how this might work if we take Uta Frith's view of autism[9] and examine the kinds of behaviour we would predict resulting from such a deficit in understanding meaning and developing a theory of mind.

A failure to understand how others think and feel would lead to:

- A difficulty in predicting behaviour, perhaps leading to finding people aversive.
- A lack of empathy and poor emotional expression.
- No understanding of what others can be expected to know which in turn will make language pedantic or incomprehensible.
- No idea about affecting how others think or feel, leading to no conscience, no motivation to please, no communicative intent and a lack of spontaneity in interactions.
- No sharing of attention, leading to idiosyncratic reference.

- A lack of understanding of social conventions including conversational strategies. This in turn would lead to no signalling with the eyes, poor interaction, poor turn-taking and poor topic maintenance.

These difficulties will be explored later in the book and alternative 'explanations' will be offered in some cases. What this illustrates, however, is that diagnosis at the psychological level can offer a bridge between the possible biological causes which we are beginning to unravel and the actual behaviours upon which our diagnosis must be based. Without such a diagnosis we are left with a collection of symptoms with no rational explanation and we are left floundering when it comes to thinking about how such symptoms might best be treated or even eliminated.

THE CONTINUUM OF NEED

The triad of impairments characterising autism also apply to Asperger's syndrome (or the most able individuals with autism) and to those with profound and multiple learning difficulties in addition to autism. But the manifestations of each impairment will vary according to the general level of intelligence and the existence of any additional problems. Pupils with Asperger's syndrome, for example, do not suffer additional intellectual retardation although their 'autistic' characteristics do lead to particular kinds of learning difficulties. In the social area, they may fit anywhere along the continuum of 'withdrawn' to 'active but odd', although most pupils with Asperger's syndrome will initiate and want social contact, but lack the understanding and skills to carry it through successfully. The child with profound and multiple difficulties in addition to autism is likely to be at the other end of the social continuum, withdrawn into a self-stimulatory world, and attempts by others to intrude into this world may be met by aggression. It is also possible, however, to find children with profound learning difficulties and autism who do seek out others and approach them in primitive and bizarre ways, often related to proximal sensations of smelling, stroking or biting.

In the area of language and communication skills, the most apparent difference between the group with Asperger's syndrome and others with autism is the high degree of verbal behaviour, and indeed structural language skills may be an area of strength. We have recently come across a seven-year-old boy with Asperger's syndrome who had taught himself to speak four foreign languages from tape–book packages; he was able to generalise what he had learnt (i.e. he did not just repeat verbatim the exercises in the text he had learnt) so he had clearly mastered each language and not just a series of set phrases. However, communication remained a fundamental problem as it does for all individuals with Asperger's syndrome. This young boy, for example, would suddenly decide to switch to another language in his mainstream playground and seemed to have no awareness that others would not be able to understand him.

The child with additional profound learning difficulties, however, is likely to be mute and sign language will prove almost as difficult to acquire. What little communication there is will be of the most basic kind, usually learnt responses to meet basic needs. Often it is the teacher or the carer who is putting all the effort into the communicative exchange, just as a parent does with a young baby. The child may scream or cry in response to his or her own needs (hunger, frustration, pain) but without any realisation of the effect on others, and it is the person who responds to that scream 'as if' it meant that the child wanted something out of reach who is interpreting the scream as having communicative intent.

The rigidity of thought and behaviour is still apparent in Asperger's syndrome although it will manifest itself in more complex ways than in the pupil with autism and additional learning difficulties. Obsessional interests are more a feature of Asperger's syndrome than simple repetitive actions or stereotypes, although these too may appear at times of stress. The more profound the additional learning difficulties, the more likely are stereotyped and self-stimulatory activities to occur and this is even more so when there are also sensory disabilities.

One further difference between pupils with Asperger's syndrome and those with more classical autism lies in motor development, the pupil with Asperger's syndrome being likely to be ill co-ordinated and often having delayed motor milestones. This applies to both gross and fine motor skills and the pupil with Asperger's syndrome may be described generally as 'clumsy'. This may have implications for some teaching approaches. It also has interesting connections with dyslexic-type problems which we will discuss later.

DIAGNOSIS AND SPECIAL EDUCATIONAL NEEDS

It is currently fashionable in education to decry the value of a diagnosis and to look at the pupil's interactions with his/her environment as a way of determining special educational needs; indeed there is a tendency to leave 'within-child' factors out of the equation altogether. We would argue, however, that an understanding of the fundamental difficulties faced by a pupil at the psychological level is crucial to developing a curriculum and a teaching approach that addresses that pupil's needs. Responding at the level of behaviour only, may lead to unhelpful or even damaging misinterpretations of the pupil's behaviour and a consequent failure to identify the true educational needs.

Education is a social activity and as such it is fraught with misunderstandings for the pupil with autism, but also for the teacher of such a pupil. Unless the teacher is aware of the difficulties engendered by autism, behaviour may be misinterpreted as rude or lazy and the child either labelled as having emotional and behavioural difficulties (if there are no general learning difficulties) or said to be unmotivated with a short concentration span, or labelled hyperactive and classed as having severe learning difficulties. Thus, a declared wish not to label a child because labels are stigmatising and lead to low expectations does not result in the child being label-free and the behaviour being dealt with in a value-free way. It is part of our human condition to categorise and interpret behaviour in order to make sense of it and a policy of no diagnosis may paradoxically lead to a situation where a child has a plethora of labels, each used to 'explain' some aspect of behaviour.

PROPOSITIONS UNDERLYING OUR UNDERSTANDING OF AUTISM

In this section we set out propositions which underpin our own understanding of autism. These propositions are rooted in the theoretical understandings described in the Preface, but we have taken things further in trying to formulate a conceptual framework which will not only be explanatory of autism but will also indicate a way forward in terms of education and care. We suggest that there are two key features of autistic thinking: firstly the way in which information is coded, stored and retrieved in memory, secondly the role of emotion in those processes.

MEMORY

One of the paradoxes of individuals with autism is their good, and in some cases prodigious, rote memory ability compared to deficits in their ability to recall personal events. That is, they may be able to recall all sorts of facts about the city they live in: the dates of its history, its population, its bus routes and so on but be unable to recall their walk through the city earlier in the same day. These kinds of memory problems have generally been attributed to problems in episodic recall (the recall of events) but we suggest that the problem lies not in episodic memory as such but in the '*personal episodic*' part of autobiographical memory (the memory concerned with ourselves).

Thus, the kind of difficulty we have in mind means that the individual with autism *would* be able to recall established facts about the city (because these are part of general _semantic_ memory), general semantic/categorical knowledge (about cities in general) and procedural knowledge for skills (e.g. how to get around the city on buses). There should also be little difficulty with episodes that do not include a personal element, but there is a problem here in accessing that information. Thus, if the child with autism had witnessed a car accident while out walking and had appeared very excited and interested at the time, it is often puzzling when questions like 'What did you see when you were out?' are met with silence or a bland statement about trees or the countryside, because that is the usual learnt response to that question. Yet we can show that the memory is there by prompting or cueing the response with more directed questions such as 'Did you see an accident today?', which may well be met by a recovery of the excitement of witnessing the original event.

The problem is that in order to recall episodes, we have to do so in one of two ways. One is to provide cues that automatically trigger the memory. These cues are often inadvertent ones, tied to what was happening at the time, and the memory is recalled without any conscious effort on our part. In fact, the memory may be painful and we would prefer for it not to be triggered by a particular tune, or smell (both very effective triggers for this kind of episodic memory) but we have little choice in the matter. In the same way, many individuals with autism seem at the 'mercy' of their memories as it were and many fears or examples of delayed echolalia (parroting of something they have heard in the past) may arise from this 'triggering' of episodic memories.

The other way of recalling episodes is under greater control but involves a sense of oneself. One has to deliberately think back and place oneself at the scene of the experience to recapture how one was feeling and what one was experiencing at the time. Children without autism, who are asked about what happened on their walk, can think back to the excitement they felt on seeing the cars crash and this will trigger the memory. Children with autism have difficulties in remembering themselves performing actions or experiencing events without a cue because, we believe, they have difficulty in experiencing events as happening to themselves. Temple Grandin has described this as being like watching a video of life rather than feeling a part of it at the time and it is this that gives such a qualitative difference to autistic experience.[28]

There is a sense, then, which those who work with autism will recognise, in which individuals with autism may know something but remain unaware that they know it. The memories may be present, but they are not tied to a sense of self that allows the individual to search for them spontaneously, when asked about the weekend, for example. In such a situation, children with autism will then use a strategy that we all use from time to time when we cannot be bothered to search our memories: they will use semantic knowledge about themselves to give an answer related to what they normally do at weekends. Individuals with autism have this knowledge of themselves because it can be established as kinds of 'facts' and is like knowing about themselves from the outside. Their difficulty comes in experiencing themselves and thus, with no way of searching the memory spontaneously, all episodes need to be cued. Without the specific cues, they might answer the question about the weekend (in writing 'news' on Monday morning, for example) in terms of visits to a cafe and swimming (the normal weekend routine) and fail to mention some dramatic event that caused the routine to be abandoned and led to much distress at the time. In the light of this kind of example we clearly need to extend our description of the memory paradox in autism which we noted above. Individuals with autism may have good rote memories but the key feature of such memories is that they are dependent on being cued—they cannot be retrieved 'at will' but rather need to be prompted.

We need now to consider why there should be this difficulty in developing personal episodic memories. Clearly the development of personal episodic memories into a structure that can function effectively depends on the existence of an 'experiencing self' which codes events as part of a personal dimension. That is, there needs to be some mechanism that enables the individual to encode things that happen to him/her in the world in such a way as to make those events memorable for the future. And this means, not simply that they can be remembered, but that they can be recalled at will. As we have noted above, what is necessary for effective functioning in the future is that the individual can search memory at will for things that he/she needs to recall.

The implication is, then, that the difficulty is rooted in the processing of information. We should stress here that we are *not* suggesting that individuals with autism have no feelings and no self. Indeed, it seems to us that they have a tendency towards strong feelings and we return to this notion later. They also may know a lot about themselves as individuals and not only recognise themselves in photographs but may take pleasure in doing so (although there is considerable individual variation in this). But what we are saying is that those individuals have an inherent difficulty in encoding information that is present in any episode in such a way that it becomes readily usable to them in future situations. In short, they feel things such as emotions but they have a difficulty in using those feelings to reflect on them, to communicate them or to make their memory processing more effective. And it is to the subject of emotion that we now turn.

THE ROLE OF EMOTION IN AUTISM

We have just hinted at another of the many paradoxes in autism, which is that individuals with autism may respond in highly emotional ways yet remain unable to identify or describe their own emotional states or indeed those of others.

To explore this paradox we need to consider the notion of 'evaluative appraisal' as a part of the process of thinking. Such appraisal occurs when an individual makes a personal evaluation of the significance of particular knowledge and in so doing brings together realities of the world with personal interests in an intentional and meaningful way. Clearly, this is of a different order to simply having knowledge. In everyday terms, we know that we remember events not simply in terms of objective facts but in terms of how we felt about those facts; we know that we remember emotionally charged events better than those of little emotional significance. In short, the way in which we are able to reflect on our own emotional perceptions of events is an important part of how effectively we memorise and so later recall. It has long been recognised in education, for example, that mugging up facts for an examination leads to a shallow kind of learning which makes learning difficult at the time and is quickly forgotten. Yet if something is very important to us in an emotional sense then there is almost no effort involved in learning it and the learning may be so deep rooted that it is difficult to forget (we may, for example, recall every insult thrown at us by our loved one in a past quarrel).

The implication of the above is that one might reasonably look for the cause of the kinds of difficulties in searching for and recognising meaning, that are apparent in autism, within the emotional dimension of determining meaning. Without meaning which is related to how the person with autism feels about a task, then problems cannot give rise to intentional behaviour which includes a model of the goal and that person's directedness towards that goal. In essence, in non-autistic development it is emotional states that allow intention to come into being and we know that in autism intentionality is a difficulty and emotional states are 'paradoxical'.

Of course, we are talking about new learning here. Habits can be run off without emotional involvement and with very little direction of attention. It is a feature of habits that they run automatically and we are only aware of the process when they are disrupted. Thus we can drive home without any conscious awareness of how we did so, but we become immediately aware if there is an unexpected road block or some danger that draws our attention. Yet, if we tried to drive all the time with this level of conscious awareness of what we were doing, as one has to do when learning to drive, then our skilled performance would be disrupted and we would be stumbling once more over having to steer, change gear and signal all at the same time. Thus the degree of intentionality and directedness in a task is directly related to the amount of conscious control needed. But an inability to exert any conscious control means that all new learning will be very difficult and performance will largely be a matter of learned habits. This is just the situation we see in autism.

EFFECTS ON DEVELOPMENT

We have already suggested that the difficulties we describe with memory processing and within the dimension of emotionality will have pervasive effects on the individual, and indeed it seems likely that the development of learning will be affected at almost every level. To illustrate this pervasiveness we identify below three common difficulties in the learning style of those with autism.

DIFFICULTIES IN INTERACTING

The problem in relating to events in an evaluative way results in the individual with autism having difficulty in establishing the meaning of social events. Without an appraisal of situations in this way it is difficult to intend one's actions in the sense of actions directed to a meaningful end. Intentions then become limited to actions that can be directly triggered by certain stimuli and the individual will appear to be unmotivated and dependent on others for any new learning. He/she will also have great difficulty in identifying the intentions of others because without a sense of events being related in a personally meaningful way it becomes difficult to establish what is wanted by others or indeed to make sense of their behaviour in terms of a meaningful whole. The child with autism may simply be unaware of current social possibilities, rather than be avoiding them as is often assumed to be the case. What is interpreted as social avoidance or a lack of will or motivation may in fact relate to a lack of social understanding based on even more fundamental difficulties with evaluative appraisal. So, in the classroom children with autism will have difficulty in grasping the intentions of the teacher and therefore will not understand why things happen in the way that they do and, importantly, will not be able to predict what is likely to happen next.

It is possible, therefore, for the teacher to be deceived by the behaviour of the child if he/she follows the 'normal' line of interpretation. If children with autism seem to be watching you intently it may well be that they are looking for signals at a behavioural level that tell them if their actions are gaining approval or disapproval. What they are not necessarily doing is checking back to compare their original actions against their perceptions of the teacher's intentions, which is the typical non-autistic sequence of events, because they have not adequately perceived those intentions in the first place.

TRANSFER OF LEARNING

Again, the problems with memory and establishing a sense of ongoing emotional appraisal involving encoding at a personal episodic level will lead to a difficulty in searching memory for usable information. If the information is not encoded within a personal dimension in the first place then, like all rote learnt material, it remains dependent on cues for recall. Therefore the child with autism may learn how to measure the edge of a piece of paper using a ruler during a maths lesson and may 'know' that skill, but may not be able to use that knowledge to work out how to measure a piece of wood in a technology lesson. If the child is appropriately cued, e.g. 'Remember when you measured the piece of paper in the maths lesson this morning', then he/she may recall quite effectively. What is lacking, then, is the ability to spontaneously search memory for knowledge that can be transferred to the new situation. And it is this ability that is essential if effective learning is to take place in 'new' situations.

BIZARRE BEHAVIOUR

If individuals with autism are having difficulty in establishing an awareness and subsequent understanding of the intentions of others, and also of their own identity, because they fail to develop adequately a sense of an 'experiencing self' then it is inevitable that they will find it hard to identify regular features of social convention. Again, this difficulty in identification will lead to a lack of understanding. Clearly, adjusting their own behaviour in a way which is appropriate within a particular social context becomes challenging for those with autism as they will necessarily have great difficulty in relating their own behaviour to a model which they have not recognised, let alone understood.

TRANSACTIONAL NATURE OF DEVELOPMENT AND TEACHING

Human development is normally a process that is firmly rooted in a particular social, cultural context and that process is essentially a transactional one. That is, learning develops through a series of transactions between individuals. For the transactions to work there needs to be participation by both parties. We can use the analogy of the dance to understand the process. One partner has to move their body in response to, and in relation to, the movements of the other if there is to be a harmonised movement forward. Similarly, in learning, there needs to be a kind of negotiation of understanding in which the learner follows the indications of the teacher and matches them with an indication of their own growing awareness and understanding. Knowledge is not simply received; it is (at some level) negotiated. This means that it is restated, reformed, reworked by the learner so that it becomes meaningful for them.

For effective learning to take place, therefore, it is clear that there will need to be some communication in the true sense of the word. Immediately it becomes apparent that the individual with autism is in some difficulty. They will have difficulty in reading the indications of the teacher, and much teaching (as does much social interaction) depends on the pupils 'guessing' what is in the teacher's mind rather than blindly or literally following instructions. One of the reasons why most of us find it easier to learn from, and with, others rather than by following detailed written instructions is that we are able to take leaps of understanding based on our understanding of others rather than having to rely on the information stated. Of course, we not only get clues to actions from observing others, we also get a sense of shared enthusiasm and involvement which motivates our own learning. All this will be lost on the child with autism who may instead find all the accompanying social signals distracting rather than helpful. Many individuals with autism will find it easier to learn from a computer program, in fact, where this confusing social dimension is absent, where information can be presented logically and sequentially and no intuitive leaps are necessary.

CONCLUSION

One of the central themes of this book is the suggestion that by working towards the development of a personal autobiographical memory, as an explicit and pervasive curriculum aim, it may be possible to establish in pupils with autism an awareness of their own role as problem solvers. We do not claim that such an approach can remedy the fundamental deficits of autism but that it may enable pupils with autism to achieve some success in their learning, albeit by a different route. Pupils with autism need to be taught skills to survive. They may need to be taught these skills in ways that allow for their difficulties in learning and their different ways of thinking and perceiving. Where it is not possible to teach them to learn in the way that others do, we may need to develop unusual teaching approaches and to teach them compensatory skills for the areas they may never fully master. But if they are to develop ways of learning that go beyond the rote learning of skills, they need to engage in a process which involves the experiencing self in emotional appraisal; pupils need to learn to be subjective and to learn through their subjectivity. To be useful in this way, therefore, a problem used in education needs to relate to personal meanings, and the resolution of a problem needs to be seen in terms of changing or helping to establish the learners' views of themselves rather than simply changing their views of the problem. The challenge to teachers of pupils with autism is to make tasks meaningful for them, as well as helping them to appreciate the meaning that 'normally' attaches to them.

Social Aspects of Development

2

THE NATURE OF THE PROBLEM

SIGNIFICANCE OF THE SOCIAL DIMENSION

The social dimension of development is clearly of great significance in autism. At a superficial level children with autism are often described as being socially inept; at a more profound level it is clear that their difficulties within the social domain of development have a pervasive effect on all aspects of their learning and their behaviour. It is not simply a matter of them failing to learn to be sociable but rather that impairments in social development inhibit the normal social transactions that are the framework within which understandings of the world are negotiated. Also, social learning is the means by which children learn to be part of social units such as mother–child dyads, the family, the school, friendship groups and the community. These social relationships are all enabling devices that afford opportunities for further social development.

PROBLEMS FOR TEACHING

Social development is a significant issue for teachers of those with autism in that it poses particular problems for teaching. It is possible to conceive of ways of teaching, for example, self-help skills but teaching somebody to be socially skilful seems immediately more problematic. At a fundamental level the problem is that there may be some things that can be learnt (developmentally) but which cannot be taught. Importantly for us here, it appears that much of this learning has its root in learning at a perceptual (direct/intuitive) level; in normal development, none of these things are directly 'taught'. If a mother frowns at a baby, the baby is immediately upset without having to be told what the frown means or having to work it out; it is felt intuitively.

Clearly, if one could not make sense of those very basic kinds of social signals (facial expressions, eye gaze, non-verbal gestures) then one would be in difficulty when it came to building upon perceptual understandings to learn about more subtle social skills such as politeness, expressions of affection, different kinds of social behaviour in different social contexts. In short, it is difficult to imagine how one could learn social skills without social understanding. And it seems that this is precisely the position of individuals with autism. They are having to learn from the outside, what those of us without autism feel (recognise at a perceptual, intuitive level) from the inside. And it may be, then, that we cannot *teach* that fundamental, perceptual awareness of social meaning that enables social understanding to develop but what we may have to do is to teach an alternative route to understanding. We can only try to copy what seems to be the successful route for those individuals with autism who do achieve some social understanding—that is, a cognitive route.

There is the danger that breaking down social skills into conveniently sized apparently teachable 'bits' may result in social incompetence. For example, an able young man with autism had been taught to wait his turn and to offer things politely to others before helping himself. On a particular occasion there was a meeting attended by 50 people at which coffee was available from a single urn. The young man reached the urn just as someone else approached and he very politely stepped aside, saying 'After you'. This would have been unremarkable behaviour except that as others arrived at the urn the young man behaved in the same way in each case. He did not get his own coffee until the end. The point is that he had learnt this bit of socially acceptable behaviour very well but he did not have the deep understanding and subtle skill that would have enabled him to remain polite but still manage to get his own cup without waiting until the end. Without understanding, he had to adhere to the outward, predetermined form of the behaviour which then, of course, in itself became noticeable and 'odd'.

High-functioning children with autism and those with Asperger's syndrome will still have difficulty and extreme delay in understanding about mental states and this will often lead to confusion, distress and even asociability, when the pupil seeks to avoid what is not understood and is, therefore, frighteningly unpredictable to him/her. For these children, however, direct teaching may have a role to play and the teacher can try to help by teaching about mental states explicitly in clearly defined situations.

Whether or not such teaching is ultimately successful, the teacher will need, at least as an interim measure, to teach social rules of behaviour and morals explicitly and not to rely on the development of a conscience or a natural empathy. It is a common observation among teachers and parents of such children that they are reluctant to follow rules directed at them personally, where they may not see the point of behaving in this particular way, but will be happy to follow what they see as a universal rule (presumably because it helps to give structure to a chaotic world). So, rather than telling the boy with Asperger's syndrome to sit down and get on with his work, the teacher might say something like 'Everyone should sit down and get on with their work. Neil [the boy in question], will you check for me please that everyone is sitting and working?' For younger children this may have to be preceded by training in the realisation that 'everyone' includes the pupil with autism for they may well not see themselves automatically as part of a group and it may be confusion rather than disobedience that makes them fail to respond to class or group instructions.

Pupils with autism may be more appropriately called *asocial* rather than *anti-social* since they do not seem very aware of the social world around them. However, their reactions to the confusing social world may appear anti-social and the danger is that they frighten people from attempts at social interaction. The priority for such children is that they are taught how to be comfortable with others so that others are comfortable with them. We would suggest that this has a higher priority even than basic self-help skills since it will have a more profound effect on the immediate quality of life and make all future learning and teaching more successful. They may need direct teaching (a form of desensitisation) to enable them to tolerate others, and they may need direct help in controlling their own reactions to others. This may be particularly true of those with additional severe or profound learning difficulties and sensory problems. For such children, however, direct instruction is seldom appropriate, but the explicitness of social signals can be enhanced by slowing them down, exaggerating them and making sure they are received and attended to by the child.

Educationists should remember that the pupil with autism or Asperger's syndrome is unlikely to pick up social interaction skills through osmosis; mixing with normally developing peers provides great potential for learning through imitation, but only if the pupil has been taught to imitate and the peers have been taught toleration and understanding.

THE COURSE OF SOCIAL DEVELOPMENT

Before we look at specific problems and educational aspects of developing social skills we need to review the core social difficulties in autism and thus identify what it will be necessary or possible to teach (or 'enable').

TYPICAL FEATURES OF THE DEVIANT PATTERN OF SOCIAL DEVELOPMENT

There will be a delay in the development of specific attachment behaviours. What typifies social development in autism is not so much that there is an avoidance of, or a resistance to, social interactions but rather that there is an underlying lack of social interest and awareness. The child with autism may treat the adult as an object to be manipulated not out of a perverse desire to mistreat but because of a lack of recognition of human relatedness. This lack of recognition leads inevitably to abnormalities in verbal and non-verbal communication (including things such as eye gaze), and to abnormalities in initiating and responding to physical human contact.

By school age these kinds of deviations from the normal pattern of social development may become less evident but other problems in social functioning will persist. Typically, there will be a lack of reciprocity within social interaction with peers. If another child signals verbally or non-verbally that they want to take, give or share a toy, the child with autism will have difficulty in recognising clearly what the signal means and any response that he/she makes is therefore likely at best to be inappropriate, and at worst contrary to what he/she actually 'wants'. Thus many children with autism may allow toys to be taken without resistance and yet be clearly distressed at their loss, and equally they may just take what they want regardless of who it 'belongs' to or who is using it at the time. In short, if a peer should initiate a social act then the child with autism might not recognise the initiation for what it is and is therefore not likely to be able to develop it into a meaningful social exchange.

Again, children without autism learn social ways of entering into, and exiting from, play situations with others. A typical 'ploy' for joining a group is to watch what the others are doing, play alongside for a while in imitation, and gradually join in the game. The more socially skilful even learn to change the game slowly so that the group ends up playing the way the newcomer wishes, but this will not work if the newcomer tries to impose his or her will from the start. The newcomer will be rejected or the group members will become disenchanted and leave. Such learning is not made available to those with autism simply by allowing them to mix with others; imitation skills will need to be taught specifically and they will need to be taught how to pay attention, and what to pay attention to, when they observe.

SOCIAL BEHAVIOUR AND GENERAL COGNITIVE ABILITY

The more able children with autism develop the cognitive capacity to learn the mechanics of socially appropriate behaviour and therefore to some degree compensate for their initial social handicap. Even where this occurs, however, the mechanistic nature of their understanding is often apparent. Again, the writings of high-functioning individuals with autism reflect this capacity to work out social meanings and the resulting rigid application of learned social rules. In this sense children with autism can learn to socially interact, or at least can learn the routines that enable them to appear to be socially interacting; the routines that are learnt, however, tend to be those that can be learnt by rote and are not so easily or spontaneously generalisable. The teacher and carer also need to recognise that such learning takes considerable cognitive effort and can be very exhausting for the child. Normally developing children find their first days in school or nursery exhausting because of the sheer quantity of social negotiations that occur; imagine how much worse this must be for those with autism where each social negotiation is the equivalent of performing a quadratic equation in one's head.

To use an analogy, social learning in autism is like learning a second language in adulthood in a formal way. In the same way that, because of the way we are forced to learn the language and because of the fragility of our new knowledge, we might use stock, stereotyped phrases that do not involve the creation of any novel utterances, so the bright individual with autism relies on stereotyped phrases and actions in social situations. In a sense then it is almost inevitable that some of these will be used inappropriately.

DEVELOPMENTAL IMPLICATIONS OF SOCIAL IMPAIRMENT

SOCIAL-COGNITION

Clearly, if children with autism do not recognise that another person might not know what they themselves know then they will not consider the need to tell that person the 'new' knowledge. Similarly, if they are not able to recognise that they do not know something, then they cannot be motivated to 'find out'. We know that normally developing children need to attempt, at some level, to resolve inconsistencies and make sense of the various phenomena that they encounter in the physical and social world. And we know that this need drives human development along; there is a need to 'make sense' of things. Many basic child-initiated interactions arise out of the child's need to make sense of the world and that need, as we have seen from the work of Frith,[9] is not present in the child with autism.

The upward spiral of social interaction and cognitive gain that we describe above will be impoverished in autism because of the difficulties that we have identified. Regardless of arguments about which precedes the other, it is clear that in human development the social and the cognitive feed off each other and drive each other on. In our view the fundamental problems in autism, in terms of lack of social perception, will create difficulties in thinking and learning because of the way those aspects of development are linked with the social domain. Finally, it is not simply that there will be difficulties; there will also be a distinctive [autistic] style of thinking irrespective of any difficulties.

IMITATION

In normal development, dependency on adult initiation eventually disappears and so it is clear that it is not a matter of a child performing an action and then learning how to perform it socially to affect others, but rather that through imitation a child's actions are first socially bound and only later does the child learn to act independently and to elicit social interaction at will. The child with autism, however, finds it difficult to go beyond the dependency. The initial failure in interdependence leads in turn to a difficulty in acting independently and in circular fashion this then leads to failure to elicit social interactions at will.

Those who work with autism may remark here that they know children who seem to be able to imitate very accurately. The problem is that the kind of imitation that individuals with autism can achieve is of the 'exact replica' kind. The kind of imitation that is so essential to normal development is invariably active and creative, it is never an exact copy. But in autism the imitation has a parasitic quality in that the perceptual features are copied exactly as they appear to the individual. For example, most normally developing infants will turn their hands palms outwards to meet the approaching palms of an adult in order to play 'pat-a-cake' whereas those with autism appear to match the image of the approaching palms by turning their own palms towards themselves. This parasitic quality is a significant feature of the deviant pattern of development in autism and it typifies the lack of an ability to meet with the world and negotiate, though whether it is a cause or a consequence of deviant interpersonal relatedness remains questionable.

ATTENTION-GETTING STRATEGIES

An important part of the normal development of social responses is the ability to gain and direct attention. Children with autism rarely attempt to share toys or to direct an adult's attention by pointing or looking at objects. Nor do they greet others spontaneously or say farewell when they leave. They may be physically aware of the presence of an adult but the presence appears to hold no social significance for them unless the adult is the source of something they want or a signal that something is to happen. They seem unable to share a focus of visual attention spontaneously with an adult and they do not attract the attention of the adult to what they are doing or to the world around them, or check back spontaneously to see if the adult is watching their exploits. In short, children with autism have few, if any, strategies for sharing attention with others. This is not only important in social development but has important implications for teaching and learning, where such sharing of attention is often assumed, even in those with severe learning difficulties.

They appear to appreciate the use of the other person as an 'agent', as someone who can act on the world on their behalf rather as one might view a wonderfully intricate robot. The adult will be used to fulfil the child's purposes rather than being seen as someone with purposes of their own whose co-operation has to be negotiated. There will be no appreciation that the other person has a conceptual perspective that can be shared or directed. Thus, they are able to take note of another's visual perspective, but not of what they are thinking or feeling.

GAZE BEHAVIOUR

One of the fundamental mechanisms which allow social behaviours to develop is that of eye contact. It is commonly reported that children with autism show abnormal eye contact, but what constitutes this abnormality is often imprecise. What counts for normal eye contact is problematic since there is evidence to show that the contact is not so much between eyes as between eyes and the partner's face unless the contact is intended to convey particular messages of sexual attraction or hostility. What does seem to be clear is that it is deviance in the reciprocal quality of the eye contact that distinguishes people with autism from others, and not simply gaze avoidance. The child with autism, if he or she uses eye gaze at all, is not able to use it appropriately for communication. The tendency is to look too closely and too long into the eyes of the other person sometimes and not at all at other times, rather than synchronising the mutual making and breaking of eye contact.

And again, gaze behaviour has to be interpreted within its interactive setting. It is not just the behaviour of the child that develops (or not as the case may be), but also the way in which the behaviour of the caregiver to that child develops according to feedback gained in social interchanges. This is not to argue the case for a causal effect of the caregiver, but rather to suggest that development necessarily takes place within a social context and abnormal responses affect the reciprocity within that context. For example, a video recording of a mother with twins, one of whom was later discovered to have autism, shows how the mother attempts to play with both children in the same way; her failure to gain eye contact with the 'autistic' baby, however, means that the play session does not develop as it does with the normally developing baby, but instead is dominated by attempts to gain that eye contact.

BIZARRE BEHAVIOURS

Individuals with autism often behave in ways which seem bizarre. Yet it may be that there is a reason for this apparent bizarreness. Behaviour only becomes bizarre when it falls outside what we normally expect. But that is to take the adult's viewpoint; the 'bizarre' behaviour may be making sense in the child's understanding of the world. What may seem odd to the onlooker may be reasonable to the individual in as much as there is a point to his/her behaviour. An action, however obsessive, may be serving a function. That is not to say that such behaviours in those with autism should be encouraged. Indeed, it may be the carer's role to enable children with autism to manage their behaviours without using particular strategies, if they are self-damaging or anti-social for example. But what may seem logically bizarre may in fact be psychologically reasonable.

Although all children feel anxious at times and therefore produce atypical behaviours, pupils with autism are unusual in the kinds of events that lead to anxiety. It is this that makes their behaviour appear unpredictable and abnormal, when in fact they are reacting in typical ways in response to extreme anxiety. Therefore recognising the source of the behaviour is likely to be the most fruitful step in helping the child to manage and control that behaviour, as we discuss later.

DEVELOPING PEER RELATIONSHIPS

There is typically a gross abnormality in the relations a child with autism has with peers. The marked absence of co-operative play means little reciprocity in relations with peers and considerable time spent unoccupied or in stereotyped activity. Few people with autism make personal friendships of any depth although some develop a network of associates who share a similar interest. Lack of empathy often results in increasing isolation as they get older. This may seem sad, and indeed it is from our perspective, but it is also an important facet of the deviant pattern of development that typifies autism. It may not be a source of sadness for the individual with autism, who might prefer to be left alone. This poses an ethical dilemma for the teacher and carer about the purpose of intervening to impose a particular pattern of social behaviour which might not be wanted by the person with autism. Yet it is important to ensure that when an individual with autism is alone and without friends, that this is a meaningful choice and not a by-product of not knowing how to go about making or maintaining friendships. Only when we have taught these skills can we be sure that the decision to play alone is a real one.

Friends are not important just as social companions, however. Friendship groups are important because it is these that, in the normal pattern of development, serve as contexts within which basic social competencies emerge or receive consolidation and elaboration. So, for example, friendships enable the development of social communication, group entry and co-operation skills, the social control over impulses, self-knowledge and self-evaluation and knowledge of skills to be used in, and attitudes about, the world. They also form a bridge between dependence on the adult-dominated rules of social behaviour that dominate early childhood and the knowledge that these rules can be bent or adjusted for different circumstances that allows for more independent functioning as an adult. In western cultures at least, it is the rebellion against adult rules that comes with the support of peers in the teenage years that leads to the development of our own views on life and behaviour as autonomous adults.

Therefore children with autism have to develop their behavioural patterns (and work through their problems) without the benefits of the social learning contexts of friendship. Thus they are doubly deprived; they appear to have an inborn difficulty in establishing social skills and then this difficulty means they are denied access to the very contexts in which such skills are practised and elaborated. Teachers need to be aware of this, not just so that they can assist children with autism to form friendships, but so that they can try to compensate for these missed opportunities when friendships do not develop.

LACK OF SOCIAL AND SYMBOLIC PLAY

Children with autism are typically characterised as exhibiting impoverished play behaviour and a failure to learn by imitation, as noted above. Those with additional learning difficulties may engage in simple manipulation of objects but not in functional or symbolic play. Their play is typically stereotyped and repetitive rather than symbolic or imaginative. Even with the more able where there is often some form of functional play and even pretend play, the latter is repetitive and invariant. Also, as we saw above, they engage only infrequently in peer interactions, so shared play is rare or non-existent, except for 'rough and tumble' and chasing.

Interestingly, their levels of social interaction increase and their levels of solitary activity decrease when they encounter non-autistic children over a period of time so, again they are clearly affecting the social environment and being affected in turn by it. However, evidence shows that there are not likely to be significant increases in the frequency of verbal communication or appropriate play unless there are direct attempts to teach this. Some of the more successful interventions in encouraging play behaviour in children with autism have come from situations of 'reverse integration' where normally developing children are recruited to play with those with autism. This can be enhanced by teaching the normally developing peers how to play with those with autism or setting them specific objectives. One interesting project gave normally developing children the task of observing the characteristic 'play' behaviour of individuals with autism (however stereotyped this was) and then devising a game incorporating that activity so that the child with autism would have a familiar task when learning to play with others.

NEGATIVISM IN SOCIAL INTERACTIONS

Certainly, normally developing children seem to be predisposed to comply with adults' requests and adults, therefore, often interpret actions as showing negativism when in fact the child with autism is unable to comply through lack of attention or lack of ability to reflect on the situation. Children with autism may lack the predisposition to comply in as much as they lack the understanding of the social situation necessary to enable them to respond appropriately. In this sense they might be better described as 'non-compliant' rather than 'negativistic'.

WAYS OF FACILITATING SOCIAL DEVELOPMENT

ATTENTION TO OTHERS AND JOINT ATTENTION

Much of the work on directing eye gaze to objects of joint attention has not been done within the social skills training framework, but rather in the area of general teaching approaches. Structured teaching approaches such as those of TEACCH (developed by Eric Schopler and Gary Mesibov[20]) often start with getting the child to attend to the task in hand which is often measured by eye gaze, or even more crudely, head turning. However, it may be that some individuals with autism receive information better from peripheral rather than central gaze vision, and so it may well be better to allow the individual to demonstrate their own way of 'looking' at a focus of attention.

Work on vocatives or touching to gain attention is generally done on a differential reinforcement basis, with limited success. In this approach the child's attempts to address someone without first gaining their attention (e.g. the child just starts talking without eye contact, gesture, or vocative to indicate who is being addressed) are ostentatiously ignored at first and then attended to with mock surprise and comments such as 'Are you speaking to me? You didn't call me or look at me so I didn't know'. The results of such procedures are that the child may be able to learn that he or she must get attention in certain circumstances but is usually not able to generalise this learning to other situations.

In our experience the most productive way to begin to teach joint attention is to start as in normal development by noticing where the individual is looking, or what the individual is doing, and commenting or interacting with that, so that joint attention is ensured. The important point is not to try to impose one's own agenda but rather to follow the lead of the child; he or she has to learn what an interaction is as well as what a particular interaction means. This means that time spent letting the child establish his or her own starting point is not wasted if it brings that child closer to an understanding that they do have a starting point and that it is something that can mean something to someone else. In our view it is possible to use a child's particular obsessions or stereotyped actions as a legitimate starting point. This is not to suggest this as a way of encouraging the obsession but simply that one has to engage with what is engaging the child whatever that may be (within the bounds of decency and safety, etc.).

Alternatively, the teacher needs to remember that joint attention can never be assumed just because it seems obvious to us that we are referring to the object pointed at or held out for inspection. Instead, the teacher needs to give explicit instructions (verbally, through signs or symbols, or by highlighting the object in some way for the child without any language) on what to look at, and to teach such skills as looking at pointed-at objects, directly. This will be explored further in the chapter on communication.

TEACHING GAZE BEHAVIOUR

It is possible to spend a lot of time selectively reinforcing the use of eye gaze to gain attention but the success rate is likely to be limited. The most fruitful attempts are likely to be those where the purpose of gaining eye contact is immediately apparent and relevant to the child, such as, for example, making eye contact contingent on being allowed to do something that the child wants to do. In such situations, eye contact may be avidly sought even by those who normally 'avoid' it. Again what this emphasises is that it is not the 'knowing how' of the skill that is lacking in autism but the 'knowing when' and the 'knowing why'—areas that are far more fundamental and difficult to teach. Again, if teachers are not careful, all they will achieve in teaching eye gaze, as suggested above, is a rather bizarre set of responses on the part of the child that will be inappropriate in the majority of social instances.

It is possible with older and more able individuals with autism to use videos of social situations such as greetings or practice interviews to get those individuals to recognise social failures or abnormalities in their own behaviour, particularly in relation to features such as use of eye gaze, and to then attempt to adjust them. If using this technique, the teacher needs to be prepared to help the individual with any negative feelings about themselves that may be generated along with any increased understanding.

Eye gaze increases naturally in certain activities, even with those with autism, and games involving rough-and-tumble activities are a good starting point from which to develop this skill. The adult can point up the significance of the eye gaze by pausing at climactic moments in the game and waiting for eye gaze to occur before continuing. Finally, there is some evidence to suggest that if the adult increases imitation of the child with autism then eye contact increases, and this may be another reason for engaging in this useful strategy.

TEACHING TO REDUCE BIZARRE BEHAVIOUR

A thorough functional analysis of the situation is probably the best initial
step. Clearly, the teacher needs to try to determine what is triggering the
behaviour and what is maintaining it. This then may give a clue to the
situations that are causing stress and to the functional value of the response
to that individual. In the past there has been a tendency to ignore this
functional aspect of the behaviour, to classify it as deviant and to attempt to
eliminate it, often through the use of blanket aversive techniques. But
clearly, such techniques do not resolve anything for the pupil, and in the
long term they probably do not do so for the teacher either. The behaviour
may need to be tackled on a number of fronts, but long-lasting effects can
only be gained by tackling root causes not symptoms; symptom suppression
will only provide a short-term solution and in the long term may make the
problem worse. This is dealt with further in the chapter on managing
behaviour.

TEACHING TO DEVELOP PEER RELATIONSHIPS

There are two complementary perspectives within this area. On the one
hand a teaching programme would need to aim towards the building of
friendships and the primary discourse skills that enable an individual to
enter a group, maintain the group topic, share information with a group and
recognise and talk about things that interest others as well as oneself. On the
other hand teachers need to recognise that these skills are going to be
difficult for the child to acquire and many may never be achieved at a
functional level; there is a need then to adjust the teaching and learning
context to accommodate the implications of this difficulty. It is necessary to
try to teach those aspects of development that would normally be 'picked up'
in the course of friendship groups while at the same time ensuring that
academic skills are not held back by insistence on learning in collaborative
groups.

Teaching towards the development of peer relationships needs to include
teaching the adolescent or young adult which rules are important to adhere
to at all times (the laws of the land and safety regulations for example) and
which can sometimes be bent or broken according to circumstances. This
is very difficult to do but it is important that they learn for example that
it might be necessary (in terms of maintaining a friendship) not to tell an
adult about a misdemeanour of a friend, as long as there are no serious
consequences for the individual him/herself.

It is also vital to attempt to teach a firm way of rejecting advances that they
themselves are uncomfortable with. This is difficult because it may be hard
to get them to identify how they are feeling and because it may fly in the face

of previous teaching that got them to tolerate advances and gestures of affection from others. We need to remember that there will be no peer group to share anxieties with or to establish group norms of behaviour.

It seems to us that a legitimate aim of a teaching programme (in the area of personal relationships) might be to encourage reliance on peers rather than adults and to develop the outward signs of friendship behaviour at least. It may seem a sham to teach the outward show of friendship without the emotional attachment that usually underpins it, but to have even a superficial friend may serve a valuable function in developmental terms and be a gateway both to a wider social life and to further social understanding.

At the same time, it is important to note that mere placement in mainstream or non-specialist schooling will do little of itself to ensure friendship groups. More able children with autism or Asperger's syndrome are often isolated, teased and even bullied and the teacher needs to be alert to the very real distress this can cause even when the pupil does not fully understand what is going on. Teachers will need to teach 'friend' behaviour directly and will also need to prepare sympathetic peers in ways of befriending the vulnerable pupil. Pupils may also need to be taught directly and explicitly to work out rules amongst themselves rather than always applying to the adult as arbiter and to make decisions to 'break' minor rules such as eating a snack before the proper adult-designated time. These situations may need to be contrived, with the other pupils acting as stooges, but they are necessary if the pupil with autism or Asperger's syndrome is to learn to make decisions rather than rigidly follow rules.

Even within specialist schools, however, such problems need to be tackled explicitly. Peter was a 13 year old with autism and additional moderate learning difficulties. His speech was limited to short phrases and was often echolalic, both immediate and delayed. He co-operated well with adults and was dependent on them to structure his learning both in academic contexts and in social situations. Peter attended a specialist school and boarded there on a weekly basis. His parents tried to increase his independence from them by integrating him into a leisure club for individuals with learning difficulties (most of whom did not have autism) at the weekends and during the holidays. Peter had coped with this as long as he was being directed by an adult, and he was interested in other children but rather nervous of them; he was not popular with them. His parents felt that he was lonely and they wanted him to have a friend whom they could invite round to visit him at weekends and in the holidays.

The problem was identified as having two main components: there was the problem of finding ways of involving Peter in sociable activities at the weekend to keep him occupied and prevent him from becoming lonely, and there was the problem of helping Peter learn how to make friends. The first problem was more easily resolved. The family advertised for a voluntary schoolboy helper to befriend Peter and they selected an 18 year old in his last year of schooling before going to university. This young man spent some time visiting Peter in school and finding out about him and about autism. He then went on short outings with him alone and began to visit him at weekends. He spent some time in the weekend club with Peter, helping him join in the activities, and took him swimming and on country walks. Peter's parents bought a tandem so that he could go cycling with his 'friend' and the young man also took Peter to the cinema, to a disco (for people with learning difficulties) and taught him to play simple card games.

Peter's life changed dramatically in that his weekends were now busy and his relationship with his brothers and sisters improved now they no longer felt under pressure to entertain him. They would sometimes accompany Peter and his friend on cycle rides or trips to the cinema and so family outings became much more possible even when the friend was not there. Although the young man became fond of Peter he had to stop visiting regularly after a year when he went to college, and there was some regression during the period when a new volunteer was being trained to take over. However, Peter soon accepted the new 'friend' and that part of the problem has been tackled successfully.

Although it might have been easier to teach 'friend' behaviour with peers who did not have autism, for practical purposes it was decided to teach Peter how to make friends during his time at his special school. The first step was to make Peter less dependent on the adults around him and more dependent on his peers. For a start all activities that Peter enjoyed were made into joint activities at some point. Thus, Peter could not go swimming until he had found a partner to accompany him, he had to choose a 'friend' to go to lunch with and to sit next to when he was there, he had to walk within touching distance of a chosen partner when going for a walk in the country (he was not made to touch, but from time to time he had to check that if he put out his hand he could touch his partner). Then new activities were introduced that required a partner. For example, Peter's class was taught country dancing and new board games were introduced.

Once Peter had got used to sharing activities with a friend, attempts were made to make others more attractive to Peter so that he would want to be with them spontaneously. Peter and his peers were given more of the power that had previously resided with the teacher or classroom assistant. For example, they took turns to be the one to say when to go to lunch and to give out drinks and biscuits at snack time; the daily 'monitor' would also be the one to give out stickers for good work (identified by the teacher first, in this case). In this way, Peter became much more interested in his peers and the combination of the increased power given to peers and being 'forced' to accompany one another to activities resulted in Peter spontaneously 'choosing' someone to do something with on occasions. This was not always successful, depending on the partner chosen, but Peter soon learnt who was most likely to reward his advances and so some kind of 'natural' friendships began to emerge within the class group at school. This was carried over into leisure activities in the evenings.

TEACHING TOWARDS SOCIAL AND SYMBOLIC PLAY

There is evidence to suggest that individuals with autism can learn to develop some aspects of symbolic play over time and that this can be accelerated when given instruction. It is necessary not only to teach the child new symbolic ways of playing but also (through the use of reflection) to teach him or her to be aware that they can play in this way, if the child is ever to learn to do so spontaneously. In the successful integrated play groups it is perhaps that the other children are 'cueing' the symbolic play behaviours and so the child with autism is enabled just to join in.

There may remain children with autism with additional learning difficulties where the effort needed to teach such play is great and where teachers wonder at the value of teaching a skill which cannot be called a survival skill, when there is so much else to be taught. There is no way that anyone outside the situation can or should set the priorities for the teacher, but we need to bear in mind that even the outward show of symbolic play could make the child more attractive to other play partners and so might help a process of integrative play from which so much else may be learned.

TEACHING TO REDUCE NEGATIVISM IN SOCIAL INTERACTIONS

As Wendy Brown (a pioneer teacher and principal in the education of pupils with autism) has said, the child with autism likes to do what he or she likes to do. And this truism addresses one of the central features of autism, that the individual resists changes in routine and engages in repetitive stereotyped behaviours. The appearance of negativism, therefore, usually emerges when any new behaviour is introduced, although it is not always a form of resistance to the new; it may be a protest at the old and boring. Another feature of autism seems to be a reluctance to repeat things on demand (presumably because they do not see the point and have no desire to please) and so a failure to respond to a problem that has been successfully tackled in the past may just be a failure of motivation.

Similarly, children might revert to a primitive strategy (such as picking up the object nearest the right hand each time) because they have forgotten or never really knew that they have another way of responding. They are waiting for the teacher to cue the correct strategy because they lack the ability to spontaneously search for problem-solving strategies in their repertoire.

As with bizarre behaviours, the teaching remedy for all these cases will depend on the initial detective work in isolating the 'cause' of the negativism. In most cases the actual remedy is obvious once this has been done. So the social skill of being able to get by in the world without using apparently negative behaviours can only begin to be developed by the individual with autism when the teacher begins to understand how to interpret individual behaviours.

TEACHING SOCIAL SKILLS THROUGH THE CURRICULUM

TEACHER–PUPIL RELATIONSHIPS

There have been special curricular approaches based on asocial methodologies, including the use of computer-assisted learning, for some aspects of the curriculum. These may be a necessary step in some instances to avoid holding back academic progress, but there should also be a parallel programme of teaching the child how to learn in social contexts. It may be, however, that the teaching situation needs to adjust as much as the child (which is possible at least in specialist settings) and that some teaching approaches such as Low Intrusion Teaching[21] (where the teacher acts as an unobtrusive facilitator rather than in a directive way) and the Option approach[13] (where the child is put in control of the learning) are more facilitatory than others, at least for certain children at certain times. Against this, has to be set the well established successful practice of over 20 years of specialist teaching, which has shown that most gains are made through positive intervention on the part of the teacher. Methods such as Low Intrusion and Option are useful where the need is to develop spontaneous behaviour and to allow the child to be more in charge of his/her own learning.

However, more directive methods may be needed where the priority is to teach an important life skill and in such cases the visual structure of the environment, with the use of visually documented programmes that can be referred to for each stage in the task (as developed in the TEACCH programme[20]) will help the child to tackle tasks independently without having the extra difficulty of coping with simultaneous social demands from the teacher. In a more extreme version of this principle, computer-assisted learning can allow the child to master academic or cognitive tasks in an environment free from social distraction, although there will also need to be specific training in generalisation of these skills if they are to be applied in real-world situations.

Although the common finding is that individuals with autism will need one-to-one teaching to develop new skills, there are approaches (such as that employed by the Higashi School originating in Japan[21]) that teach entirely through the group and where group conformity is the main teaching aim. Such approaches are often successful (at least in a selected sample of individuals with autism) in training social co-operation and ridding the child of idiosyncratic and disturbing behaviours, but they have not been shown to increase understanding or to enable independent functioning without the supportive group structure.

CO-OPERATIVE AND COLLABORATIVE LEARNING

The prime fact to remember is the maxim that a child should not be expected to learn more than one new thing at a time and that levels of difficulty within a problem should not be increased within more than one dimension at a time. For example, John, a 16-year-old child with autism and no expressive speech, was able to both read and write (at a simple level) in the classroom situation. However, when he was required to go shopping with a list, the additional difficulty of the new social dimension made it impossible for him to use his reading ability and he became distraught. What he needed was to have a more direct and accessible list, in the form of pictures of the items to be bought, until this particular social dimension became less threatening. As teachers, we need to be aware of different dimensions of task difficulty and to recognise that these dimensions will affect children across a range of their accepted abilities. This will be dealt with more extensively in the chapter on thinking skills.

The teacher must be clear on the teaching priority for each child; if it is a new skill or area of knowledge then this is probably best presented to the child individually in one-to-one teaching or through computer-assisted learning. If, however, the priority is to teach co-operation or collaboration then the task given to the group should be familiar (at least for the child with autism) so that the new and difficult social aspects of co-operating or collaborating can be focused on. The teacher needs to be aware of the difference between teaching group behaviour (i.e. how to behave in groups), teaching through group interaction (where some degree of co-operation or collaboration is needed to complete the task) and teaching in groups (where the only benefit of the group is that the child learns to concentrate on and complete a task in the distracting presence of the group). All three ways of using groups may be valuable in teaching pupils with autism, but the teacher should be clear about the goals and limitations of each learning and teaching context. The ever present danger is that teachers feel the need to be teaching something new in the collaborative learning situation whereas, for the child with autism, the learning that is new is how to relate to others.

TOWARDS LESS DEPENDENCY ON TEACHERS

There is a need to put individuals into situations where they can reflect on their own role in problem solving. We have used instant photographs both to help our pupils to reflect on their own role in situations and to act as cues to enable them to carry out tasks on subsequent occasions, independently. The problem comes, of course, when the pupils become as dependent on the photographs as they were previously on the teacher.

One way of reducing dependency on adults is to get individuals to rely on their peers and this may be achieved by structuring situations so that peers have degrees of 'power' and control. It may also be possible to develop more independent learning styles through a cognitive curriculum where the child is given access to, and made aware of his/her own use of, a range of strategies for problem solving. In contrast, certain teaching approaches within a behavioural framework may actually foster dependency on adults (or on aspects of the programme). The situation here is obviously unclear in as much as attaining some skills at a behavioural level may lead to an increase in possibilities for independent learning while attainment geared to short-term specific rewards is unlikely to lead to self-motivating, self-directed future learning. At the very least, behavioural approaches to learning should include a period of 'overlearning' and a programme for generalisation and the transfer of skills.

Programmes such as TEACCH, while being very structured, usually include a programme for independent learning (at least independent of the adult, not of the structure). In this programme the child is put in charge of his/her own timetable that is coded in a way that indicates where a task is to be done and with what degree of supervision or help. The child is taught basic work skills as a matter of routine, where to start a task, how to proceed systematically, always to complete work started and so on. In a sense, this kind of idea is a concession to the autistic way of thinking; what is created within TEACCH is an autistic environment where the individual with autism can then function. Clearly, the danger is that the individual does not learn to function in the non-autistic environment (learning does not necessarily transfer out of the particular structured environment). Within the TEACCH programme itself this problem is addressed by a 'cradle to grave' service. There are important fundamental issues here about the necessary features of an 'educational' programme and about acceptance and potential.

CONCLUSION

Reciprocity in social interactions seems to be the way to achieve successful relationships and that is a skill which children with autism do not seem to develop. Reciprocity involves the individual in learning to attend to social cues, and to interpret and respond to such cues correctly (and appropriately, in terms of ever changing social scenarios). There is, then, a high level of cognitive load in social situations. And if we can reduce the cognitive demands of the task by familiarity or through increased structure, then people with autism may be enabled to be (or appear to be) more socially competent, to exhibit a higher level of social skills. It is not possible then to consider effectively social behaviour and social skills without taking into account the cognitive demands of the situation. For example, it may be that children with autism relate better to adults than to peers simply because the adults are more predictable and more prepared to structure the situation, thus making fewer cognitive demands on the child.

It seems that we are designed to be very sensitive to basic social and interpersonal signals. We respond to other persons abstractly through imagination, expectations, and conceptualisations based on prior experience. But we also respond directly through the pre-conscious, pre-wired assessment of smells, movement, patterns of facial expression, sounds and touch. Individuals with autism fail, to a greater or lesser extent, to send, or respond to, many social and interpersonal signals of this kind. They may send uninterpretable or unpredictable signals, and they may misinterpret the complex signals sent by others.

To those with autism developing social skills is a fundamental matter. They are having to learn *about* social development rather than simply learning to develop within a social context. They may be having to learn by rote the incredibly complex set of social rules, which are in part perceptual as well as socially created. It is little wonder, then, that their learning of social skills may not seem to generalise in the way that we might expect.

To learn all of the ever changing rules by which we conduct our social lives, in the way which may be necessary for those with autism, must be like trying to learn a complicated dance, when you do not know what dancing is, when you cannot hear the music, and when, just as you have managed to imitate one step of your partner's, you find that the dance has moved on, the rhythm has changed and so (perhaps) has your partner. What teachers and carers need to do, it seems, is to slow down the dance of social development. We need to give our partner with autism time to learn one step before we go on the next and we need to make that step clear and to show how it is part of the whole dance. And, perhaps most importantly, we need sometimes to follow a movement that our partner makes and interpret it as if it were a step in the dance, as if it were a social act. Because by doing that we let our partner feel what it is like to be dancing, that is, what it is like to be engaging in a social interaction.

And above all we need to try to understand the problems that our partner is having in learning to dance and to remember it is the process of dancing itself that he/she is having to learn, not merely the steps of a particular dance.

Emotional Aspects of Development

3

THE CENTRAL ROLE OF EMOTION

The question of an emotional difficulty underlying autism is one that is open to misunderstanding and controversy. At one level there is an acceptance, which dates from Kanner's original description,[17] that 'affective disturbance' is characteristic of individuals with autism. All descriptions include some notion of the child being 'withdrawn', 'aloof', and 'unattached' to people, at least to some degree. Yet there has also been a strong route of psychological research and theory that has neglected exploration of the emotional disturbance in autism, preferring to see it as secondary to other more cognitive deficits.

Some of the reluctance to view the emotional disturbance as central to autism arises from an association of that view with the view that autism is psychogenic in origin, 'caused' by faulty parenting. Kanner, while describing the features of the disorder with an accuracy and a perceptiveness that has largely stood the test of time, thought the condition was an emotional illness. Mothers of children with autism were described as 'refrigerator mothers'. Some workers in this area have defended this position but research and clinical experience over the years have failed to provide any evidence that mothers (or indeed fathers) 'cause' autism. If there is a causal link with parents it is more likely to be through the genes than through the method of child rearing.

It is also clear that emotional disturbance often follows from developmental difficulties and it is logical to suppose that a failure to understand about mental states, for example, would lead to people seeming confusing and frightening and this in turn could lead to withdrawal and a failure to engage with people. It is only those aspects of emotional development that require understanding of emotions as mental states that are disturbed in autism; actual feelings are not disrupted. As we will show later, this is an explanation that fits many of the facts of emotional development in autism, and yet there are unanswered questions. As we have already noted, if the normally developing child does not reach a full understanding of mental states until four years of age, then a question mark hangs over what accounts for the differences in emotional development that are apparent between the child with autism and the normally developing two or three year old.

Hobson[11] sees the prime deficit as an emotional one in that the child with autism is not able (because of some unspecified biological disturbance) to perceive the emotions of others and thus fails to develop a sense of shared, and then later different, perspectives on the world. His view is that this sense of connectedness with others (which he terms 'intersubjectivity') is not something that we learn in a cognitive way through coming to understand about mental states in the abstract and then reasoning about the mental states of others. Rather, we perceive it directly and from this grows an understanding that there is a difference between the world 'out there' and how that world is perceived by us, and that our attitude to the world enables us to perceive it in different ways. From this perception, the normally developing child develops his or her own attitude to the world, responding not just to how things are, but to the meaning they hold for us (something to eat, something to play with, something to share with others). The child's sense of meaning comes from the first shared meanings, so a disturbance at the earliest emotional level will lead to the kinds of cognitive difficulties in understanding mental states which are seen as central in autism.

THE COURSE OF EMOTIONAL DEVELOPMENT

PERSONALITY DEVELOPMENT

Individuals with autism do develop characteristic ways of behaving, but those ways are often characteristic of a number of individuals with autism. This is necessarily so, in that autism is defined by the existence of these same characteristic behaviours. Thus, because of this and because of the much reduced or non-existent social interaction in individuals with autism, their individual personalities may not be so apparent. However, the individual with autism is an individual first, and it should be remembered that the individual is expressing that personality in his or her actions and that the effects of autism are modified by that personality in each case. Nevertheless, the personality of individuals with autism is problematic in that the development of their own sense of self is impaired; their 'consistency' is rooted in fundamental physical, perceptual reactions and tends not to relate to differing interpersonal contexts as is the case for individuals without autism.

There has to be some endurance over time if a feature of an individual's personality is to be described as a 'trait'. Yet some attributes may seem to endure because we use the same label for what are in fact very different behaviours. For example, to use the term 'cruel' to describe a child of three pulling off the wings of a fly and the same term to describe that individual, when he is 33, humiliating his wife, does not necessarily mean that we have identified an enduring trait of 'cruelty' in that individual. The causes and the motivation for the behaviour may be very different at the two different ages. When we come to consider the teaching of social skills to individuals with autism, we will need to recognise this distinction between enduring personality traits and particular behaviours, both in our conceptualisation of the problem and in the way in which we deal with it. In terms of autism, we need to be wary on two particular fronts. Firstly, we will need to challenge the common view that experiences of early life must determine adult character; we know that such experiences may influence but this is very far from determination. Secondly, we must beware of describing a behaviour as if it were automatically a personality trait. It would not be accurate to call someone 'aggressive' simply because they show aggressive behaviour in a situation where they have not been taught other ways of having their needs met. Such labelling is unhelpful within the positive teaching approach we advocate.

Within normal development there are two periods of pair bonding: mother–infant and male–female, both of which are normally biologically determined. A biological disturbance might therefore disrupt bonding at these critical developmental stages and this may well be the case in autism, particularly during the first period. The mechanisms for achieving the other forms of co-regulated behaviour (e.g. imitation and symbol use) also appear to be key deficits in autism. Thus early personality development may be affected because it is not based in interpersonal relatedness; the child with autism responds not so much to the actions and attitudes of the other as to specific forms of stimulation. Therefore in autism, the bonding process is either disrupted or it fails to develop at all.

In normal development, also, imitation provides a mechanism for sharing experiences and building personality. Young children join in social games of joint imitation with their caregivers from an early age (imitation of facial gestures has been observed in the neonate) and later use it as a way of joining groups in play. Children with autism have difficulty in imitating at all and when they do it is often in a very mechanistic way.

DEVELOPMENT OF SELF CONCEPT

The notion of self concept that we are employing here suggests that it contains:

- The descriptive element which is often termed the self picture or self image.
- An evaluative component which is frequently referred to as self-esteem, self-worth or self-acceptance.

A transactional view of the development of self concept would suggest that it arises out of the influences of 'significant others'. That is, you interpret yourself in relation to how others behave towards you. And, as it arises, the self concept also actively shapes the way the child interprets experiences.

If the sense of self arises from these intersubjective experiences, then it will be severely disrupted in autism. If we are right in our views, then the first part of the self concept (the self image) should be only partially affected since it is possible to build up a self image from autobiographical facts about ourselves that we can learn from exposure to certain situations and from what we are told by others. Thus, individuals with autism may know what sex and age they are, where they live, what they like to do and so on. But they will have more difficulty with anything that depends on their own experience of things and on knowing what it feels like to be the kind of person they are. The second aspect of self concept is liable to be totally absent in autism. Lacking a sense of themselves they will be unable to reflect on their self image and make value judgements about it. Nor are they liable to notice the reactions of others to them (as opposed to their behaviour) so they will be unable to incorporate these judgements into a sense of self-esteem.

Yet there are some individuals with autism (typically the more able) who do seem to display the characteristics of having a low self-esteem and of feeling undervalued. It is necessary to be certain that we are really witnessing self-esteem in these cases. Very often what is expressed is a dissatisfaction with the way they are being treated or with the fact that they feel unable to tackle certain tasks, expressed in a way they have learnt to use without full understanding. That is not to deny the reality of the depression that may accompany such expressions but we should not misinterpret their use of certain expressions as necessarily implying the same thing as if individuals without autism were to use them. Nevertheless, some individuals do seem to develop a sense of self-esteem (unfortunately, in our experience, usually a low sense), often based on a failure of their own expectations of themselves or the reactions of others. We should take account of this in working with pupils with autism and be aware that we need to demonstrate explicitly that we value them, even when we are disapproving of their actions, for they may not have the sense of themselves, or our underlying attitudes, that would enable them to make that inference.

Thus, in spite of their marked difficulties in understanding others, children with autism will nevertheless respond to the way they are treated and it is important for adults to show that they value and respect the children clearly so that there is not undue pressure for the child to change. We need to distinguish between wanting and needing to change behaviour (a distinction that is made quite clearly in the Option philosophy[13]). If those working with individuals with autism can accept and value their pupil without the need to change him/her, then this will free the teaching situation of tension and allow both teacher and pupil to concentrate on actually changing the behaviour.

LEARNING ABOUT EMOTIONS

It can be misleading to think that children with autism will necessarily be withdrawn from society. Children with autism may be attached to their mothers or they may not be, they may be somewhat sociable or not sociable at all; some may express a wide range of emotions, others may express little emotion.

Yet there is a qualitative difference in autism (necessarily so, by definition of the condition) and the attachment to others may not be motivated by the usual emotional bonds but because of the way that person behaves. In a confusing world, where people are unpredictable, it is not surprising if the child with autism clings to what he or she knows. The more that person (usually a parent) makes themselves predictable to the child and behaves consistently, the more the child is likely to depend on their help in negotiating the world and to rely on them for a source of security. That is love, albeit not as other children might feel or express it, but it also allows for the feeling that parents of children with autism often get (regardless of how 'attached' their child seems to be) of being treated as objects. It is also a sad fact (for the parents, rather than the child) that children with autism may be as, or more, attached to some object as to their parents.

Sharing attention will be dealt with more fully in later chapters, but there is evidence that children with autism do not naturally or spontaneously look where others are looking or pointing or direct their gaze to objects that are held out to them for inspection. The interesting fact is that if this ability is tested it can be found to exist in children with autism, at the right level of intellectual development. In other words they can follow the direction of someone's gaze or a pointed finger if they are specifically directed to do so. The fact that they do not normally do so relates to their lack of emotional involvement with the actions of others and it has tremendous teaching and learning implications, especially in relation to communication. In the same way, pointing does not often develop spontaneously in autism and children with autism often do not direct the attention of others in any way except to have their own needs met.

The way in which the normally developing child learns about the emotions of others is still a matter of debate. It is likely that there is a biologically endowed facility for recognising emotion in others and for the sharing of a sense of connectedness with others. There may, however, be mechanisms through which this is achieved and the identification of these would be very helpful when considering teaching such an ability. It is possible that the empathetic process may be achieved through the imitation of the outward signs of behaviour such as crying in sympathy or smiling in response to a smile. Certainly these behaviours occur early in normal development and are notably disturbed in autism where children may grimace when being taught to return a smile and may find the sound and sight of someone crying highly amusing. The role of emotion in theory of mind development remains contentious.

The normal pattern of the development of social and emotional understanding is disrupted from the outset in autism although some more able children with autism come to some understanding of the rules of social and emotional life without fully understanding the underlying emotions. They are more likely to be able to identify facial expressions of emotion that are relatively straightforward, such as happiness or sadness, than emotions such as surprise, which implies understanding of mental states (that someone had an expectation that turned out to be wrong). But it is not just mental state knowledge that causes the difficulty in understanding emotions in autism. Individuals with autism have difficulty in recognising the full picture of emotional expression so that they cannot match facial expressions to appropriate body postures and gestures or to tones of voice or likely settings. Their own use of gesture is limited to 'instrumental' ones (pointing at something wanted, for example, or warding off someone's approach with an outstretched hand) and they do not spontaneously show comfort gestures or give indications of their own embarrassment.

They also have difficulty in identifying their own emotions and talking about them. The teacher or carer needs to be aware that what may appear as a convincing explanation of how they feel and why, may simply be the application of what they have learnt to say, without full understanding. Wendy Brown has given an example of a pupil at her residential school who was crying pitifully one day. A concerned adult asked her what was wrong and received the reply that she was sad because she was missing Simon. Now this could have been a very acceptable explanation since this pupil was extremely attached to Simon and liked to sit next to him on all possible occasions. The only thing that stopped everyone getting excited at this wonderful breakthrough in emotional understanding was that Simon happened to be standing next to the pupil at the time. The most likely explanation is that Simon had been on holiday some time before and the pupil had been upset on some occasion during this period. Someone had assumed a connection and said 'Poor Katy, I expect you're upset because you're missing Simon' and this now became for Katy something she could offer as an answer to the perplexing question about her emotional state which she did not understand. None of this is to say that Katy's emotions were not real and probably had a reason, but it is to point out that someone who does not understand about emotions may nevertheless pick up some of the 'correct' expressions to use and it is only those who know the child well who will not be fooled by glib responses.

Temple Grandin offered a further illustration of this when being interviewed on television. The presenter had got her to talk about her childhood and her many outbursts of anger, pain and frustration when she reacted to loud noises or unpleasant sensations with emotional rages. The presenter probed Temple to discuss her emotions further by asking her what she had felt like when all this was happening. Temple began to talk again about the feel of material on the skin, when the presenter interrupted to say 'No, I mean what did it *feel* like emotionally'. There was a pause when one could see that Temple was aware of the meaning of these words, she knew what she was being asked but the question was literally unanswerable for even this most able woman with autism, since she could not reflect on her feelings, and she had not learnt to bluff (or lie). She finally got round the problem by saying she had been too preoccupied with the way things felt and the pain caused by the sounds and so on to worry about how she was feeling.

When it comes to understanding how one is affecting others, the same caution needs to be shown in interpreting the behaviour of individuals with autism. It can sometimes seem to parents or teachers that a child with autism is particularly good at getting under their skin and knows just how to irritate and annoy others. The point to remember is that as normally developing children grow up and become more socialised they move from dependence on more basic ways of relating to others to more culturally determined ways, using symbolic systems such as language. It has been shown that mothers can identify their own babies by smell, but the fact is that we tend to suppress this knowledge; the mother does not generally enter the nursery and sniff around until she can locate her baby but relies instead on the way her baby looks, sounds and behaves to identify him or her and to assess how the baby is feeling. We reserve some of these primitive ways of knowing one another for intimate situations between mother and baby or between lovers, but our general social relationships are not conducted through smelling, licking or stroking, at least not in current UK culture.

If children with autism are not socialised into these cultural understandings, then they are liable to be more responsive to these more primitive indices of how people are reacting. Thus, they may not be able to perceive and recognise the emotion but they may react to it in the sense that they may quite literally smell the fear that we are trying to conceal (as we try to ignore challenging behaviour, for example) and they may get excited by the tension they feel in the suppressed anger.

Donna Williams is another able young woman with autism, who has written an account of her early experiences.[33] She is able to go and talk to groups of people internationally and yet may still go into a room and touch all the furniture before sitting down. When asked why, she has said that she cannot get a sense of where things are from just looking at them, but needs to touch them to establish this, just as a blind person would. We need to remember this in teaching, when we might be tempted to just dismiss certain behaviours as meaningless and bizarre; they might well have a vital meaning for the child. We may still need to eliminate or at least limit some behaviours such as smelling armpits when greeting strangers, to enable the child to be acceptable in the wider world, but we should ensure that we have understood the function of that behaviour for the child and have taught the child a more acceptable way of gaining the same end.

When teachers talk about emotions in autism, it is often not the lack of emotional expression that is of concern but the uninhibited expression of emotions, especially negative emotions. It is the inability to control emotional outbursts that can be a problem, whatever the level of intelligence of the child, and this is one of the instances where the more able child with autism usually fares worse. Children with additional severe learning difficulties might be excused an emotional outburst because it is easier to accept their lack of understanding. But attitudes to the child with good academic and intellectual ability are likely to be less understanding because it is harder to accept that this area of development can be so out of keeping with other areas.

It is important for the teacher to realise that the developmental age of a pupil in terms of emotional understanding may be less than a few months, while at the same time bearing in mind that that pupil's experience of life and the learning that has taken place will mean that his or her behaviour and understanding are not directly comparable to those of a young baby. This has implications not only for the teacher's attitude to the emotional outburst but for the method of dealing with it. If we simply direct our energies to stopping the behaviour we should be aware that we are not only setting the child a very difficult (if not impossible) task, but we are preventing the development of any further understanding of emotions.

If the child knows no other way of expressing that emotion, then preventing that one way of expression is in effect saying to the child 'You must not have this emotion' or at least, if you have it, you must not show that you have it. A preferred way of dealing with the situation is to show the child that you recognise the emotion being expressed and to help the child to identify that emotion too, through words, or by showing the child itself in a mirror or taking a photograph or video recording that can be reflected on later. Then we can demonstrate, with words if appropriate or through actions, other ways in which the child can express that emotion. This then ceases to be a matter of the child having to suppress the emotion (which would be very difficult for anyone, especially if the emotion is strongly felt) and becomes one of having to change the way in which he or she gives vent to that emotion. This is a much more manageable task and, at the same time, the child is being taught something about the emotions he or she is experiencing which is of additional educational benefit. All of this is particularly important to bear in mind where the need to control behaviour may dominate and the equally important educational task of teaching about emotions may consequently be missed.

THE ROLE OF EMOTION IN LEARNING

EMOTION AS A FACILITATOR OF LEARNING

The formal education system has traditionally underplayed the role of emotion in learning. The view seems to be that too much emotional involvement is a bad thing and that emotions will disrupt learning, which in turn is seen as a logical, objective affair. We now know that this is not true except for the most abstract kinds of learning and even there gifted mathematicians only seem to succeed where there is real passionate involvement with their work. We know from our own experience how easy it is to learn about something we are deeply interested in and conversely how difficult it is to apply oneself when we find the material dull and boring and where we cannot see the connection with our 'real life'.

It is also suggested that one of the functions of emotions in humans is to allow for creativity and novelty in our responses to the environment, so that we are able to tackle problems we have not encountered before. As we will see later, in the chapter on problem solving, our normal response to problems is to try tried and tested methods of solving them, but if these are blocked, or the problem is new, we experience emotion (fear, anxiety, excitement, depending on the level of the challenge and what there is at stake). This emotional state enables us to escape from our habitual ways of thinking and acting in this situation and to bring other possible courses of action to our attention.

While young normally developing children approach life with a seemingly insatiable curiosity, the situation in autism is at once different and more complex. To begin with there is seldom this natural curiosity and zest for knowledge on which to build. A feature of autism, after all, is the lack of a need to make sense of the world. However, teachers could do more to build on the interests that are there, even if they do not seem very productive. It might be easy to follow the example of Temple Grandin's teachers and let her develop her interest in architecture and design, while it might be more difficult to think of useful extensions to the ability to balance bits of fluff on ledges so they just tremble but do not fall when the ledge is tapped. The young lad concerned with the latter activity (and some related ones, less palatable to relate and even more difficult to use) did not have the intellectual or verbal ability for this to be extended into physics; in any case he did not seem to care why they balanced, only that they did. His interest was channelled into 3-D art projects with some success but, although these were more successful in terms of joining in with class lessons and fulfilling a part of the curriculum, it cannot be claimed that they developed into anything that added greatly to his quality of life and in any case, left to himself, he still preferred his bits of fluff. We mention this because we do not want to pretend that it is always easy to follow glib instructions like 'Take a child-centred approach' or 'Follow the child's lead', but we would claim that you are more likely to be successful if you do try to do so and work with the child's interests rather than against them.

Not only is there likely to be no emotional engagement in a task in children with autism, but also there will be none of the compensatory motivations that operate with normally developing children. The child with autism will not understand about pleasing teacher or parent, although he or she may learn what to do to produce favourable results or to avoid trouble, and will not be motivated by the long-term goals of success or a realisation of what will be needed to gain future employment and manage one's life (the concept of delayed gratification cannot develop where there is little ability to predict what *might* happen). Without that emotional engagement, it will be difficult for the child to engage in spontaneous or creative work because that requires some appreciation of the meaningfulness of the task (dependent in turn on an emotional appraisal) and learning will become dependent on what the teacher or the environment prompts the child to do.

EMOTION AS A DISRUPTION OF LEARNING

The teacher has to be concerned not only about emotional engagement with the task, but also with emotional reactions to task performance. There will not be one right way to teach children with autism across all situations and individuals. It may not be possible, or desirable, to deal with the emotional reactions to failure and encourage a problem-solving approach to all the tasks in a day. The majority of day-to-day activities are most sensibly learnt using small steps and structured prompts so that the child knows what to do without stress and can perform the task as a habit without directing undue attention to it. But if *all* the learning is of this kind then new tasks or changes in the situation, or failure of learnt routines, are all likely to cause extreme emotional distress, which leads to a level of anxiety which blocks further learning.

Although some stress is necessary and helpful for learning, as we saw above, too much stress is simply disruptive. What is more, this kind of scenario, where disruptive reactions are simply managed or blocked, means that the child is not being equipped to deal with other such situations in a more productive way. Even if it is only for a short period a day, or even a week, the teacher needs to set aside some time to actually tackle this situation and teach the child how to cope with failure (a small failure at first, of course, in a task where there is not too much emotional involvement) and use the emotions productively.

In considering the role of stress in learning, the teacher also needs to be aware of the very many different causes of stress in autism to ensure that these do not reach unmanageable proportions. One common source of stress relates to the size of the teaching space and the density of occupation. The sense of what is a comfortable distance between themselves and others (proxemics) is often very disturbed in all forms of autism. At the least disruptive level this may just mean not being aware of a socially appropriate distance and standing right in front of people and talking into their faces; this will merely require social training, although it is very difficult to teach the kind of sensitivity to social intimacy that determines the appropriate distance. More disruptive of classroom life are pupils who are themselves made acutely uncomfortable and anxious by invasion of their 'private' space and especially where their private area is very extensive. Teachers need to be aware when their own presence (perhaps with the best intentions of leaning over to express interest or offer help) is causing unmanageable stress, perhaps even panic.

They also need to be aware that other pupils can create the same sense of stress and fear merely by their presence, if the room is crowded or there is a lot of 'free' activity going on. This is especially noteworthy in open-plan classes operating on an integrated day schedule, where pupils are free to wander from one activity to another. Many more able pupils with autism or Asperger's syndrome do best in more formal settings where the classroom space is ordered and free movement is limited. However, the teacher's awareness of the problem and dividing up the room into clearly marked areas can help the child with autism to cope with less formal settings (awareness of the problem may mean, for example, explaining to the pupil the informality of set parts of the day in formal terms). Similarly, any kind of group work is likely to prove stressful.

Other potential sources of stress may arise from the general stimulation of a busy classroom and the teacher needs to be aware of the particular 'triggers' for any individual child. For one it may be level of noise, or a particular noise (e.g. the sound of chalk on a squeaky board), or it may be the use of a particular word or phrase. We have known a child fly into a rage and start biting herself whenever the word 'no' was heard even if the teacher had meant 'know', so it can be difficult to monitor one's speech all the time.

A classroom can also be a very distracting place, especially if there are stimuli that relate to a particular child's obsessional interests. The way the sun shines through a particular window, for example, may be a source of compulsive fascination, as may the presence of a sink in the room for a child obsessed with water. Some distractions may be inevitable, and the child will need to be taught to cope with these, but there may be others which can be removed or the classroom arranged to obscure them in some way.

FACILITATING EMOTIONAL DEVELOPMENT

As was discussed at the beginning of this chapter, there might be some aspects of emotional development that will need to be taught directly to children with autism. It is possible, at least in principle, to teach *about* emotions, for example by using situations in which the child is clearly experiencing an emotion and helping the child (through talking about it or by showing them their facial expression in a mirror) to reflect on that experience. However, not all aspects of emotional development can be tackled in this direct way and then it may be a matter of facilitation rather than direct teaching.

FACILITATING ATTACHMENT

There have been behavioural attempts to teach some of the behaviours associated with attachment such as mutual eye gaze. These have been successful in getting the child to gaze mechanically into another's eyes but, since there is no understanding of the purpose of eye gaze and no motivation to do it spontaneously, this has been shown to be a rather sterile skill. Such mechanical training may in fact increase the social awkwardness of the autistic behaviour.

A promising teaching approach is that of 'Interactive Teaching'[23] which has been used with individuals with profound and multiple learning difficulties who were not formally identified as autistic but whose behavioural descriptions leave little doubt that this was the case. The basis of the approach is to relearn the fundamental, earliest social interactions. This is done by creating a situation between the teacher and the individual with autism that mirrors the early interactions of a caregiver and infant. By slowing, simplifying and emphasising these to the point where some pleasurable response is obtained from the individual, it is possible to build upon that response so that the individual is put in charge of the interactive routine and is thus able to stop, continue, extend or change it at will. This is a very useful approach to establish the beginnings of interpersonal behaviour in those individuals who are very withdrawn or who have additional severe learning difficulties. It seems to us that the medium (e.g. touch, music, sounds, words) for this kind of interactive teaching might vary between individuals and is dependent, in part, on their level of functioning but that the principle would remain the same.

The Option approach[13] does not specifically claim to affect 'attachment' but, since its goal is the development of normal functioning, it clearly has relevance here. Again, its rationale is that one should go with the child and incorporate the child's actions into an interactive format which, like early dyadic interaction, puts the child in charge. The teacher acts with such high levels of energy, enthusiasm and excitement (while always responding to the child's indications when he or she has had enough) that the children should have their attention caught and begin to share some of these emotions. Two 'success' stories are well documented but there has been no systematic evaluation beyond the observational study of one of the authors.

Music-Assisted Communication Therapy[21] uses music to emphasise and reinforce pro-social behaviour in dyads of either a child and teaching staff or child and parent. The music must be live so that it can be continuously responsive to the child's actions but the teacher him/herself may produce the music (usually by singing) when no musician is available. This has its problems but could also have advantages in increasing the saliency of the interacting individual. The idea is that the child's responses are mirrored and incorporated into musical routines which the child finds easy to memorise and which help to make the interaction more predictable and thus less stressful or frightening. Musical interaction also helps the child to pace the responses and thus contributes to the flow of the social interaction, breaking through the child's difficulties with social timing.

DEVELOPING A SELF CONCEPT

Including self-recognition as part of body awareness teaching is a common curricular practice, for example body-part recognition and mirror work with make-up or hats. It is also possible to use tickling games such as 'Round and round the garden' to distinguish self from other: once the child has learnt to anticipate a tickle at the climax of a rhyme, he or she can be helped to perform the actions on the adult and appreciate that in those circumstances it is the adult who gets the tickle at the climactic point.

At a more central level of self-recognition, being aware of the self as an intentional and problem-solving ego, much of the cognitive approach that appears in later chapters is directed to this end. This approach uses structured periods of reflection during and following problem-solving tasks to try to make learners aware of their own role in the task and the strategies that they have employed.

DEVELOPING EMOTIONAL UNDERSTANDING

Social skills teaching using video feedback can be used to address this issue with the video being used to draw the child's attention to the facial expressions and bodily postures of him or herself and others and the circumstances that have led to the emotional expression. This will only work where the emotions are sufficiently unambiguous for both the child and the teacher to be certain about the emotion being displayed. This is liable to be the more unpleasant emotions such as anger or distress since the expressions of pleasure are more ambiguous and it is harder to predict the situations that will make one person happy than to predict ones that will lead to anger. This may mean a reversal of the teacher's normal instinct to play down unpleasant episodes in favour of using them as teaching aids. Although videos give a fuller picture of the emotional expression and the situation that has led to it, many children with autism will find a video recording as complex as everyday life and are unable to isolate particular events such as relevant facial expressions. In that case instant photographs or still video may be useful, at least initially.

It may also be helpful if the teacher or carer always expresses emotions unambiguously, drawing the child's attention to the way the adult is feeling and labelling the emotion expressed. Thus the adult may say things like 'Oh, you looked at me then Amy; that's lovely. It makes me very happy when you look at me. See how you've made me smile Amy, because I am happy that you looked at me'. This is the kind of approach used in Option and we suspect that many teachers in the UK would find this rather embarrassing and artificial. We need to remember that it is artificial to the extent that all other groups learn such things naturally and spontaneously and do not have to be taught in this very direct way. Embarrassment may go as it becomes part of the normal teaching routine.

In spite of the difficulties of working in groups the more able children with autism at least may develop some emotional understanding through the experience of a group dynamic. This can be fostered through regular 'counselling' sessions in which group members try to identify problems they are experiencing (particularly in relationships) and others are encouraged to help find ways of resolving those difficulties. Clearly this is something that needs careful structuring but useful results can be achieved in terms of their understanding of personal relationships and their role in those relationships.

PARTICULAR EMOTIONAL PROBLEMS

SEXUALITY

Given the problems we have identified in self-awareness and emotional understanding, it is clear that individuals with autism are going to have particular problems functioning as full sexual beings. It appears that a significant minority will not be aware of themselves as sexual beings at all and for this group, in consultation with parents, it is probably better that sexual interest is not explicitly developed. There will be another group who have no interest in others sexually but have clear sexual needs and then it is the teacher's (and carer's) role to ensure they have a means of expressing their sexual needs (i.e. know how to masturbate) and that they are able to follow (if not always fully understanding) social rules for privacy and discretion. It may also be appropriate to teach 'waiting' for an appropriate time and place by teaching distracting or sublimating behaviour.

Others (generally the more able) will be interested in a full sexual life, although this may not be because of full sexual interest so much as wanting to be the same as others. This will involve full sex education but there are ethical problems in that the teacher might have to come to terms with the fact that some individuals might never develop caring relationships with others but still want to have a sexual relationship. The problem is, then, whether one should teach practice that would enhance the quality of life of the individual and be in line with accepted norms in society but which may be against the moral principles of the teacher and the values laid down by society (and the law) for schools to inculcate.

Teaching appropriate sexual behaviour, however, may not be the most pressing problem in dealing with the issue of sexuality in autism; the lack of emotional understanding also leads to specific vulnerabilities. Petra, for example, was a 15-year-old girl with autism and additional severe learning difficulties. Her speech was quite good but her understanding was limited. At a superficial level, Petra was very sociable. She liked to be touched, especially if it led to tickles, and she liked to feel people's hair—especially beards and Afro-Caribbean hair types. She would often approach people, strangers or not, and take their hands and put them on her own body. Sometimes she said nothing, although she might give an anticipatory chuckle; occasionally she said 'tickle'.

Petra had had some sex education at school but this had been limited to physical and factual matters. Petra was able to deal adequately with her own menstruation although she did not understand about privacy and would announce the start of her menstruation in graphic detail to whoever was around. Her 'knowledge' about where babies come from and how they are made had led to an interest in pregnancy (often extended to men with fat abdomens of whom she would ask, 'When is your baby going to come out?', just as she did to women) and male and female sex organs and sexual characteristics. All this behaviour suggested that Petra not only needed to learn about privacy in hygiene and sexual matters but that she would be very vulnerable to sexual abuse and needed to learn some way of rejecting unwanted advances. At the same time it was important not to frighten her into loss of contact with everyone since her interest in others had done much to increase her social responsiveness and had added to her quality of life.

A key problem here was that, like others with autism, Petra was not able to reflect on and report her own feelings. Thus, she could not simply be taught to reject advances that made her feel uncomfortable, as might be taught to other children, since she would not be able to identify (for herself or others) when she was feeling uncomfortable. The teaching therefore would need to identify rules that could be taught to Petra and which she could apply herself without needing to identify emotions in herself or motivation in others. This would necessarily make such learning rather rigid and unnatural but it was felt that this would be better than taking no action.

As a step towards making Petra's behaviour more socially acceptable and also making it less provocative, she was taught the notion of 'private' in relation to toileting and hygiene. She had already learnt to perform toileting functions in private and to make sure her clothing was properly adjusted before leaving the toilet area. She was now taught that this applied to talking about toilet issues or menstruation and that she should look for a female adult (preferably her key worker when at school, but she practised going to a variety of females according to who was available) and tell her about starting menstruating in a quiet voice. All this needed many weeks of practice both as a form of role play before the event and then with prompting and modelling after the event. It was important that the training concerned what to do rather than what not to do. If the training had centred on the negative, this would not only make it more difficult to learn the correct behaviour, but there would also be the danger that Petra would have realised that this was a behaviour with which she could control the adults around her. Thus she may have increased her 'embarrassing' behaviour simply because of its effect.

Once Petra had mastered the notion of privacy as applied to her bodily functions she was taught that if strangers tried to touch her in personal areas or talked about doing so she should say 'No' and tell a relevant adult (key worker/parent). This was accomplished through various role play scenarios. A problem did arise in that there was a difficulty in identifying who would count as a stranger in this context and in generalising the behaviour she had practised with familiar adults to future scenarios with such strangers. In practice, therefore, Petra was also taught the kinds of touching and affectionate contact that were permissible with anyone and those that she could allow with a few restricted others. This resolved the issue of identifying a stranger in favour of the more easily manageable problem of identifying intimates. For example, Petra was initially given a list of such intimates that included only her parents and younger sister. Later, she was taught that when she had known someone for a long time (defined as more than ten visits) she could discuss with her key worker whether such a person might become an intimate. Petra was told that tickling should be restricted to intimates and part of her programme involved giving her other ways that she enjoyed of making contact with people. For example, she was taught games that involved contact only with the hands such as arm wrestling and 'hand over hand'.

BEREAVEMENT

Another key emotional issue that raises particular problems in autism, is that of bereavement. From what has been said about problems with attachment, teachers might feel that children with autism would not suffer from the loss of a loved one in the way that others would, and so the child's difficulties may not be recognised or addressed. It may be true that children with autism are not attached in the same way to people as are other children, but they are often attached in their own way and their feeling of loss may be made worse by their lack of understanding, not just of death (common to all children, if not to us all) but also of their own emotional state and that of others.

Frank was a nine-year-old boy with autism and additional learning difficulties. He had a normally developing twin brother. He had no speech but could make his needs known through the use of single signs. His signing vocabulary was 150 signs but these were only used spontaneously to make requests. He enjoyed rough-and-tumble play, especially with his father. For much of the rest of the time he preferred to be left to himself and engaged in simple stereotyped hand movements.

One day when Frank was at school his father suffered a heart attack and died. Frank was taken into respite care from school and did not return home until after the funeral a week later. He had protested the change when he was taken from school to the respite centre but soon settled into the routine there, which was well known to him. Frank's mother informed the school that she did not want Frank to be told of his father's death as she would do this herself when he was home again.

When Frank returned home he initially showed no signs of distress; his mother told him that his father was in heaven and that he would not be coming back. Frank seemed to be disturbed by this but it was not clear how much he understood. When the time for his father's homecoming had passed, Frank became very upset and began banging and kicking the door and signing for his father. Eventually, Frank ran into his father's bedroom and pulled open the wardrobe where his father's clothes had hung, only to find that they had been cleared away. He then cried inconsolably as he swung the wardrobe door to and fro. This behaviour lasted for some hours and it was only with some difficulty that Frank was persuaded to have something to eat and go to bed. On waking in the morning his first action was to return to his father's wardrobe and continue his wailing and swinging on the door. He could not be persuaded to go to school in the taxi and in desperation his mother phoned the school for help.

Talking to Frank about his father's death had little impact on his behaviour and attempts to distract him were only partially successful. Once the teacher and his mother had finally persuaded him to go to school he was fine and he remained calm on returning home but, as soon as the time came when his father normally returned, Frank would rush to his father's wardrobe and begin his wailing once more. A meeting was called to discuss the problem with all concerned and it was concluded that Frank appeared not to be missing his father in a total sense but in the sense in which his father was most salient to him, i.e. as a playmate in his rough-and-tumble sessions after school. This was not in any way to minimise the reality or extent of Frank's distress, but it did suggest a way forward in helping him overcome his grief.

A young male social worker, who was attached to the school, returned home with Frank each day from school and engaged with him in the kind of rough-and-tumble play that he had previously had with his father. This worked very well; Frank was very happy to play with the young man until after the time when his father used to return home. When the game then stopped, Frank accepted his supper, bath and bed without trying to get to his father's wardrobe or showing any other signs of distress. After two weeks of this the social worker instituted a game of rough and tumble at school before sending Frank home in the taxi, one day a week. Frank accepted this, and then gradually this became two, three, four days, until Frank was having all his rough-and-tumble sessions at school and was showing no signs of distress at home.

It seemed as if Frank was 'over' his distress at his father's death, although his mother reported that from time to time he would go into his parents' room and open the wardrobe and stand looking forlornly at the empty space. Some two to three months after his father's death, when his mother had started visiting friends again, Frank appeared to develop a new obsessional behaviour. Wherever he was he would rush up the stairs and make attempts to get to the attic or roof space. There appeared to be no particular trigger for this behaviour and if he was successful in entering the attic he would look around for a while and then become upset and angry, even hitting out at his mother if she tried to draw him away.

At a review meeting called to discuss his progress this problem was aired. No one could guess at the source of this behaviour until the twin brother was talking about how he talked to Frank about their father's death, 'I always tell him that he's up there' he said, pointing to the space above. The people at the meeting realised that Frank's interpretation of 'up there' was attic space, and his apparent new 'obsession' was a search for his father whenever he found himself in a new building.

Clearly, there are significant difficulties in helping a non-verbal child such as Frank to come to terms with bereavement. At one level it appeared that he was only missing his father's behaviour. At another level he was also aware of him as a person and was trying to search him out. In relation to this second level all one can do is to show understanding of his natural distress and try to deal with confusions that may arise through our use of language. Death is a topic that attracts many euphemisms and even the verbal child with autism may become confused by the suggestion that a loved one has 'gone to rest' or 'joined his Father in heaven'. For verbal and non-verbal children the following principles should apply:

- Try to compensate for aspects of involvement with the loved one as far as possible, e.g. the rough-and-tumble sessions with Frank.
- Use simple clear language to talk about death and illustrate it from natural experiences, e.g. plants/insects dying.
- Do talk about the deceased even at the risk of upsetting the child; grief is natural at loss and it is healthier to allow the grief an outlet. For the non-verbal child, photographs could be used to help with this remembering process.

CONCLUSION

Emotion is clearly a central issue in autism. Children with autism by definition have difficulties in recognising emotions in others and in themselves. In this chapter we have treated emotion as a part of the problem of educating within autism but also as part of the solution. We have suggested that emotion needs to be seen not just as an area of difficulty that children with autism have, but also as the route through to successful teaching. The role of emotion in learning needs to be recognised and thereafter its necessary function within teaching needs to be addressed.

Learning without emotional involvement seems to be limited to the learning of rote habits or skills, dependent on prompts from a teacher or from the structure of the setting. If our aim as teachers is to produce flexible, independent learners, we believe we have no choice but to try to tackle the emotional difficulty in autism and to see emotion as a potential enhancer of learning and not just as an optional extra or even a disruption.

The Development of Communication

4

THE NATURE OF THE PROBLEM

Difficulties with language and communication have always been seen to have an important role as one of the defining features of autism. The range of language skills in individuals with autism is wide and, if we consider the full autistic continuum, it is clear that the fundamental problem is that of communication, rather than language per se. Non-verbal forms of communication are affected and, in Asperger's syndrome, structural language ability may be good while communication and the social use of language remains poor.

Children without autism do not have to develop their own communicative conventions but are socialised into an existing system. Early communication is characterised by 'transparency' where the intentions and beliefs are open, not hidden. Children with autism do not seem able to recognise these mental states and so for them early communications are opaque rather than transparent. This in turn means they miss the process of socialisation through which further communicative conventions are made clear. The normal developmental pattern whereby communication precedes language and is the prime means for learning it, is disrupted in autism. This not only makes it more difficult to acquire language (in terms of meaning and use rather than structure), but it also means that there are problems for the child with autism in the way in which language is used in education. There the general assumption is made that spoken language follows communicative understanding; schools are therefore not equipped to teach the early stages of communication and their use of language builds on what is assumed to be already present. This assumption is erroneous in the case of autism.

THE NATURE OF COMMUNICATION

Communication is most usefully seen as involving some notion of communicative intent. Thus it rules out the unintentional communication that may result from physiological reactions (for example, the 'smell' of fear), from natural social adjustments in body posture or position (for example, how close one stands to people, leaning forward in interest, folding one's arms in 'defence'), or from unthinking adoption of cultural values (for example, how one dresses for social occasions). Of course one can use these normally unconscious markers consciously for communication and then they become intentional. Also, where the unconscious norms of a culture are not adopted, it is often assumed that this is intentional. This latter assumption creates difficulties in autism, particularly for those more able individuals in whom the lack of perception of social conventions may be misinterpreted by peers and teachers.

Communication usually includes a 'marker' that indicates the intention to communicate and even young pre-verbal babies making a request have to indicate not only *what* they want but *that* they want. Thus, babies will point to what they want and will use intonated sounds to indicate that they want it and they are not just pointing it out for mutual attention. At another time, the baby's intention will be to share attention and then there will be a different form of intonation accompanying the pointing gesture to signal the different communicative intent.

But intention to affect another's behaviour is not sufficient to get at the essence of communication. We can communicate with another without affecting behaviour at all, by simply affecting that person's beliefs or emotions. This distinction is crucial when we come to consider the particular difficulties in communication in autism, where the individual may learn to communicate in ways that affect another's behaviour (e.g. being able to make requests) but has little understanding of communication that affects mental states.

The same kind of problems arise when we look at the necessary and presumably sufficient conditions for communication to occur. Chris Kiernan and his colleagues[19] have defined these as:

- Something to communicate about (an awareness of one's needs and concepts).
- A means for communication (spoken language or some alternative).
- A reason for communicating (an environment that is responsive and yet does not anticipate every need).

Teaching language and communication skills to individuals with special educational needs has traditionally concentrated on teaching these aspects of communication. Individuals with autism, however, are unique in needing additional specific teaching to help them to understand about communication itself, and how to develop and understand communicative intent. This will be needed, regardless of the general level of language ability.

COMMUNICATION PROBLEMS

SOMETHING TO COMMUNICATE ABOUT

Many individuals with autism will lack one or more of the prerequisites to communication. A large proportion have additional severe learning difficulties which means they have not yet acquired many of the necessary concepts, and so they will have little to communicate about. They have needs but they may be unaware of them (they lack awareness of their own mental, and even physical, states). Normally developing infants will cry or coo to express discomfort or pleasure but the nature of these vocalisations will change once they learn that someone will respond, that is, once they have developed communicative intent. In autism, a failure to recognise the communicative effect of one's own utterances even at this early stage may mean that the utterances do not change to express communicative intent. There is some evidence that babies with autism do not make the same kinds of pre-verbal communicative signals to convey greeting, surprise, demand and frustration as do all other infants, including those with severe learning difficulties. They do develop some differentiation in the signals they produce, but these are idiosyncratic, unlike the universal signals that adults seem to be tuned into. Thus, the child with autism may come to be understood only by his or her own parents or other caretakers.

A MEANS FOR COMMUNICATION

On the second criterion of developing a means of communication, additional severe learning difficulties and/or specific language problems are likely to mean that the individual with autism has little or no spoken language. Various studies have estimated that between 20% to 50% of individuals with autism remain mute. The unique characteristic in autism is that there may be an almost equal difficulty in acquiring a sign language and using and understanding gesture. Pictorial symbol systems and the use of computer-aided communication have helped individuals with autism to gain access to some means of communication but, as with sign-language training, neither has proved a panacea for the communication problems in autism.

A REASON FOR COMMUNICATION

When it comes to a reason for communication, individuals with autism may also have particular problems. In the past, and in some cases in the present, individuals with autism have found themselves in institutionalised settings which are unresponsive to their communicative needs and so they have no opportunity to develop communicative intent. Alternatively, if they are in situations where their needs are anticipated, then there is no communicative pressure on them because their needs can be met without any communication.

LACK OF UNDERSTANDING ABOUT COMMUNICATION

There are individuals with autism at the more able end of the continuum, or with Asperger's syndrome, who do not have any of the deficits named above and yet suffer the communication problems typical of the disorder. It seems that these individuals may have the skills necessary for communication but they lack the knowledge of when and how to deploy them; in short, they do not understand what communication is about. And here we need to go back to our earlier attempts to define communication. If we took a definition that only concerned affecting the behaviour of others, then we might not see any failure in communication in these able individuals with autism. Most of them learn to 'communicate' in the sense that they do something intentionally to affect someone else's behaviour. But, unlike normally developing children, they use a very limited range of functions, typically of an asocial kind.[15]

Further analysis suggests that it is not so much that all the social functions are missing since some individuals learn to request not only *things* from others but also social routines such as chasing or tickling games. What appears from studies such as that of one of the authors is that the only functions that develop spontaneously in individuals with autism are the instrumental ones, those concerned with affecting others' behaviour, not their states of mind. For example 'request' develops whether it relates to a thing or an action but 'comment' does not develop. In order to comment one needs to have a desire to have the listener think about, or have a mental reaction to, the subject of the comment; in other words, one needs to be aware that others do think and feel and not just act.

Thus, the majority of pupils with autism are likely to have a wide range of communication problems but the ones that are fundamental to autism as such, and so shared by all those with autism no matter how able, are those that require understanding of mental states.

TEACHING ABOUT COMMUNICATION

IMPUTING MEANING

A programme to teach about communication may mean going back to the very early stages of communication where the caregiver imputes communicative intent to what are in reality mere responses to the baby's own states and thereby teaches the baby what it means to intend. However, it is not just that the child with autism has missed these experiences and needs to go back over them; autism is a biological disability which means that the child is not 'programmed' to recognise the social signals inherent in communicative exchanges. Therefore it is not enough to go through early stages of development again; the process has to be made explicit.

A good example is the fact that children with autism do not share joint attention with others by automatically looking where others are looking or even where they are pointing, but they can do this if they are specifically instructed to do so. Teachers, then, must be aware of this need for explicit instruction so they can say, for example, 'Look at what I'm holding up' before talking about it and not assume that the mere (communicative) act of holding something up means that it is necessarily the focus of regard.

UNDERSTANDING INFERENCE

In the same way, pupils with autism will need to be taught to notice the different ways things are said and the gestures, facial expressions and body postures that go with different meanings (indeed it is noteworthy that many pupils with autism learn more easily from the mechanical voice of a computer where such nuances are not present). At the same time, academic learning can be accelerated through computer-assisted learning or written instructions because the child is not having to decipher simultaneously all the confusing messages conveyed through natural speech. Most of our understanding comes from understanding people, and we respond to what we infer the *speaker* means rather than what the words mean. But the child with autism lacks this natural inferential process and will have to learn that words have more than their literal meaning; they will need to be taught how to infer what the speaker means which in turn requires that these normally implicit processes will have to be made explicit.

COMMUNICATIVE FUNCTIONS

Teaching the least able individuals with autism a verbal or signed label for an object is unlikely to lead to success in using that 'label' unless prompted in some way. Alternatively, it may result in inappropriate use as the individual runs desperately through his or her repertoire of learned (but meaningless) actions or sounds in the hope of hitting on the one that will give him or her what is wanted in this context. Children with autism need to be taught how to use and understand the labels they are given, which means they must be taught communicative functions. Request is often the best communicative function to start with since it is the earliest, and sometimes the only, function acquired by individuals with autism and it is the one whose meaning is easiest to demonstrate.

Undesirable behaviour can often be treated as a communicative attempt. The individual may be at the stage where outbursts are a simple reaction to need without communicative intent at all. However, the teacher can use such outbursts to impute the communicative intent of a request (if that is what the situation suggests is appropriate) and teach the individual to grab; if the individual already tries to grab (or grabs the teacher's hand and 'throws' it at the desired item) then the communication training starts there. Teaching the individual to stop and look at the teacher, by interrupting the 'grab' sharply with a restraining hand (and thus usually causing a momentary glance at the person causing the obstruction) can be built on until the individual gives that checking look spontaneously when reaching for the item. This can be extended to a variety of contexts and, once it is secure, the grabbing hand can be gradually shaped into a point until the individual has the communicative act of pointing and looking. Teaching pointing, without these preliminaries to teach the meaning, will only lead to meaningless pointing, which might occur even when there is no one in the room to see the point.

In our view the teacher also needs to give communication priority over behavioural conformity. Thus, merely getting the child to ask politely for something that is in front of him/her teaches cultural forms of polite behaviour but does nothing to help the child understand about communication. In fact it assumes that communicative understanding is already there. The child with autism needs to learn to ask for something when there is a reason for doing so and not just as a mechanical habit. The desired item should be clearly in the control of someone whom the child must then ask in order to obtain it (for example, on a high shelf, or locked away when that person has the key). The teacher may need to 'engineer' many of these situations throughout the day.

SPECIFIC PROBLEMS IN COMMUNICATION

PROXEMICS AND BODY POSTURE

Proxemics refers to the way in which we position ourselves in relation to others, including the 'comfortable' distance at which we conduct interpersonal relations. Clearly this will vary according to degree of intimacy and particular cultural norms, but individuals with autism appear to have difficulty in understanding intimacy and perceiving and using the social rules of interpersonal conduct. This may seem a social problem, but when social rules are broken there is an assumption that this is done with communicative intent. The individual with autism may be giving unwitting communicative signals of which he or she needs to become aware. Going too close to strangers to speak to them or peer at their faces may be taken to be an unwelcome attempt at intimacy or an aggressive threat, especially if the pupil appears competent in other ways, as many more able pupils with autism do.

Body postures not only convey information about personal intimacy between individuals, but also convey moment-by-moment reactions to the communicative exchange. It is common observation that the body posture of individuals with autism is abnormal, especially in social situations. They tend to hold their bodies tensely (which may of course be a natural reaction to the psychological tension induced by the social interchange) and not to alter posture to express interest, or its obverse, or any subtle variations on these attitudes. For example, they tend not to nod in approval and encouragement nor to signal when they wish to take a turn by leaning forward. Some of this may be because they are not in fact monitoring the exchange but, even where they are clearly interested, they may lack the skills to communicate this interest to others. Body postures that convey emotions in any conventionalised form are also a great source of difficulty. They can understand and use primitive displays of emotion such as temper tantrums or outbursts of exhilaration (literally jumping for joy, flapping with excitement) but cannot grasp more subtle forms such as frowns or nods.

The dilemma here is similar to trying to teach social skills without social understanding. With proxemics, for example, one could teach the child to conduct social interchanges at a distance of 18 inches, which would be a useful distance for most purposes in an English culture, but when adhered to rigidly by the child this would be interpreted as rejection by his/her parents. In practice the teacher of the young child with autism usually has two priorities with regard to proxemics. The first is to break down any barrier children may have that prevents intimate contact with parents and so precludes close communication. This can be done through a programme of desensitisation whereby the adult draws closer in a step-by-step way while the child is engaged in some enjoyable activity and where the steps are so small that the child never becomes anxious about the approaching intrusion. Alternatively, the adult may engage in some highly intrusive game, which the child nevertheless enjoys (such as rough and tumble, involving tickling) and introduce other forms of communicative exchange into this game. A similar approach is that of Music-Assisted Communication Therapy where music emphasises and encourages intimate, pro-social advances of the child towards an adult and this intimacy is carried over into communicative work outside the sessions.

The second priority is to develop a comfortable distance for teaching that does not present the child with undue stress and yet allows teaching to occur (given the restrictions on space and room occupancy that are liable to exist).

Again, desensitisation can be used to enable the child to tolerate the teacher's presence at a suitable distance for teaching, but there is the additional problem of wanting to go beyond that stage of toleration. If the child is to communicate effectively, it is important that the teacher's advances are seen as non-threatening, and that the child can approach the teacher without itself feeling threatened or seeming to pose a threat (e.g. by standing too close). As with the intrusive methods mentioned above for intimate encounters, the teacher needs to establish highly motivating games in which the child is alternately approached or has to approach others. An example of an appropriate game for this is a chasing game where the pleasure (usually shared by those with autism) comes from being approached and approaching others. For other social interchanges, it may be necessary to accept the teaching of rather rigid rules and to teach as many variations of these rules as the child is able to manage. For the more able child, the use of video can help them self-monitor these rules and to talk about what they feel or how others might feel when people stand too close or too far away.

Video is also the only real possibility for teaching about body posture in relation to themselves, although they can be encouraged to role-play situations (or to use naturally occurring situations in the classroom) in order for the body postures of others to be explained and made explicit for them. Unfortunately, overt differences between ways in which different individuals express themselves in body posture are usually greater than more subtle similarities in the ways in which the same meanings can be said to be expressed by the different individuals. It is only our understanding of these social and communicative messages (which operate at a largely pre-conscious level) that really enables us to recognise these similarities and respond to them.

UNDERSTANDING COMMUNICATIVE GESTURES

Communicative gestures are so automatic that we may not recognise when we are actually making them and could fail to take account of the lack of understanding in autism. Adults might hold up an item and ask 'What is this?' or 'Who can tell me about this?' They may be aware that people they are addressing might not know the name of the item or be able to comment on it, but it is rare for them to realise (unless experienced in autism) that the person addressed might not even know that the item being referred to is the one being held up for inspection.

Individuals with autism do not automatically look in the direction of gaze of an adult to share joint attention, as do normally developing infants, nor do they look towards the direction of a pointed finger. The fact is that they *can* do these things if they are instructed to ('Look where I am looking') but they do not do so spontaneously. And, because we are programmed to expect its occurrence we do not give explicit instructions to 'Look where I am looking!' as we pass something interesting in the train, we just say 'Look at that cow!' and then assume that the child has just been too slow to respond, or is uninterested, or does not know what a cow is; it seldom occurs to us that the child may not understand that the instruction to 'Look!' really means 'Look where I am looking!'

Other gestures with communicative intent are liable to be equally mysterious to the individual with autism. Gestures of comfort or affection, for example, may be reacted to as if they were assaults, and this can be particularly hurtful to parents who see this as rejection. In some cases the reaction may be triggered through the physical effect of the gesture, where, for example, an embrace is experienced as stifling. But, at least in part, this kind of reaction is the result of the communicative intent simply not being understood. No natural, inborn understanding of such gestures and no awareness of the mental states that generate them, means that they must indeed seem like bizarre movements without purpose or effect. A kiss on a wounded knee may be better tolerated as it may be seen to be a ritual associated with the healing of the knee and at least it is directed to an area that has meaning for the child; putting an arm around the shoulders of a wounded child, however, may appear to have no relevance to the wound and may be rejected as a further uncomfortable physical sensation. Parents will naturally be sad at not being able to comfort their child in this way, but it may help if they understand it not as specific rejection but as a reaction to bewilderment and confusion. It may also help them to learn other more directive gestures (such as the kissing of wounds) that may be better tolerated.

Clearly, the communicative gestures that relate to reference will have most impact in teaching situations, but parents may be more concerned with teaching some acceptance of gestures of comfort and affection. Direct teaching of the meaning of a gesture may be helpful, especially to the more verbally able child. The adult can explain that putting an arm around someone means you like them a lot or want them to feel better when they are sad. This can be accompanied by a brief demonstration, and if this is done sufficiently often the child will gradually come to accept the gesture and may even seek it. Other children and those with more severe additional learning difficulties might need a programme in which the adult gradually introduces touching and affectionate gestures by building on what the child is doing and finds enjoyable.

GAINING ATTENTION

Just as children with autism fail to notice the object of another's attention unless specifically directed to do so, equally they show their lack of understanding of the communicative process by failing to gain another's attention for their own 'communicative' attempts. This is illustrated by the child who repeated a request she had been taught to make to an empty room, not realising the significance of the fact that the secretary was not there, and again by a less able pupil who signed for what he wanted under the table where no one could see. Here the words or signs are rituals that children have learnt to go through without understanding the point of communication. The first step in increasing understanding in these cases is to get them to ensure they have an audience for their communicative attempts and to give them strategies for obtaining this audience.

Work on vocatives or touching to gain attention has been done on a differential reinforcement basis, with limited success. In this approach the child's attempts to address someone without first gaining their attention (e.g. the child just starts talking without eye contact, gesture, or vocative to indicate who is being addressed) are ostentatiously ignored at first and then attended to with mock surprise and comments such as 'Are you speaking to me? You didn't call me or look at me so I didn't know'. The results of such procedures are that children may be able to learn that they must get attention in certain circumstances but usually they are not able to generalise this learning to other situations. Less able children may need to be taught such attention-getting strategies as a matter of routine in the hope that routine use (allied to a policy of drawing the child's attention to the results of their strategy with comments such as 'Good! You are signing for "potatoes" where I can see your sign so I know what you want') will eventually lead to understanding. In some cases, of course, the child may have found an effective way of gaining attention, but the way may be aversive (hitting, for example) and there will be a need to teach alternatives. Or the child may gain attention and then not know what to with it, so will need teaching on how to express communicative functions such as 'request' and 'comment' and when to use such functions.

UNDERSTANDING NARRATIVES

Individuals with autism have characteristic difficulty in telling a story, whether fictional or real, in a way that retains the essential features of the story line. Understanding stories poses equal problems and the only strategy used appears to be to recall chunks verbatim. Part of the difficulty in following narrative structure seems to arise from the failure to set up a mental model of the discourse in which characters have semantic roles. Future references via anaphoric pronouns are therefore lost and it is not surprising if the individual loses track of the story. Thus a story or life event in which 'Mrs Jones' is the main character requires that the listener establish a semantic role for this character with the features 'female, single' so that the use of the pronoun 'she' subsequently will have a reference in the text and will be able to be understood. Failure to do this means that it is hard to make sense of the narrative in any continuing sense since there is no main character to provide the topic for which the events are the comment. The narrative will thus lose continuity. There is some evidence that individuals with autism are able to use and understand pronouns anaphorically in this way, where the full name and the pronoun occur within the same sentence, but that they do not develop active listening that sets up and retains semantic roles across sentence boundaries.

It seems equally likely that individuals with autism also fail to keep track of their listener's mental model (or even to recognise its existence) and thus do not give the relevant pragmatic markers that would help the listeners keep track of what the speaker is saying. As suggested above, however, the linguistic skills associated with providing discourse coherence (e.g. usage of anaphoric pronouns) do seem to follow a normal developmental route and are not significantly out of keeping with the individual's level of linguistic ability. It is the social and cognitive aspects of discourse that are more significantly disturbed.

In order to talk about past events the child needs to understand how narratives are constructed as well as to have the personal memory to recall the event (which we discuss in Chapter 6). Normally developing children acquire this through the skilful and structured questioning of their parents, at the pre-school stage, that builds a 'scaffold' into which they can slot their answers. In time, this structure becomes internalised by the child and he/she knows the kind of information needed to convey to others when telling a story. Children with autism will seldom be exposed to this kind of structured learning about narratives because of their social and communicative difficulties; again, they are then doubly disadvantaged by an initial difficulty and a lack of opportunity to acquire relevant skills.

Children with autism are best taught the structure of narratives (personal events, actual events concerning others or even fictional events) through an analysis of stories. This is easiest to accomplish where the child has adequate spoken (and preferably written) language skills where the key structural elements can be highlighted systematically, but a lot may be achieved in the non-verbal child through the use of pictures or photographs. The aims are to help them to perceive the overall structure of a story, to create that structure as a mental model when they hear or read the story, and to get them to use the structure in retelling stories of their own.

Parents and teachers can begin this process by setting aside time after any event (and it may be as mundane as going shopping or having a meal) for reflection. For verbal children, this means getting them to talk about what has just happened and in particular getting them to recall how they felt about what happened. This will be difficult for individuals with autism, who have problems in recognising and talking about their emotions, but it is important to try to develop this evaluative ability since, as we have seen, memories of personal events are largely dependent on this emotional component of memory.

Of course, a full understanding of narratives is not just concerned with their structure but also with their content and this involves understanding of people. Fictional stories especially rely on understanding the motivation and intent of the characters and this in turn relies on the child's real world understanding of these mental states. As we have seen, individuals with autism will have at best imperfect understanding and at worst no awareness of mental states at all. The real world provides opportunities at least for understanding the behavioural manifestations of certain mental states (smiling when one is happy, crying when one is sad) but stories that are told or read seldom give such behavioural descriptions of the participants. Thus the child is robbed of the main source of understanding and predicting behaviour and instead is given descriptions of mental states directly that may have little or no meaning.

It is best, therefore, to start with stories that are narratives of real life events where there is more chance that the child will have developed some understanding of why and how people behave as they do from an analysis of their behaviour. It is interesting to note, that when the most able individuals with autism develop an interest in fiction, it is often science fiction. In this genre, the author often produces alien beings where the normal human intuitions about behaviour do not apply and in that sense the individual with autism is then at no disadvantage in understanding and predicting the behaviour of these 'aliens'.

Finally, the teacher needs to develop ways of helping children with autism to create mental models for themselves. However, mental behaviour is difficult to prompt or to monitor. One way of starting the process is through the use of songs (or rhymes, but songs will usually be easier and more effective). Children can be taught a song until they can sing it for themselves and then, step by step, words are omitted from the song and replaced with a gesture of some kind. The children, then, need to keep the 'missing' word in their head in order to rejoin the song at the correct place. The rhythm of the song helps them to achieve this and gives them experience of mentalising in a very accessible way.

A COMMUNICATION CURRICULUM

THE NEED FOR ALTERNATIVE AND AUGMENTATIVE SYSTEMS

Autism is frequently accompanied by additional developmental problems that will affect language. Sometimes there is additional specific language impairment and this is likely to be the case in those individuals with autism who have reasonably good non-verbal skills but remain mute through life.

More commonly, there are additional learning difficulties and, where these are severe, they are liable to limit and delay the development of language in themselves. When they are accompanied by the communication difficulties of autism, that makes it even more difficult for the child to learn a language and any additional specific language problems on top of this will increase that difficulty. Given the importance language has as a prognostic indicator of future social and educational development and later quality of life, it is clearly important that education should stress some alternative 'language' for those who are unable to acquire speech. There remains the difficulty of deciding when to go for an alternative system to speech and then in deciding which of the available systems would be best.

On the first point about when to give up on spoken language the short answer must be 'never' but that does not mean that other systems should not be taught as well. It has been shown that if children do not speak by the age of 13 then there is little, if any, chance of their doing so later. But an individual case can always disprove a general finding and this can only offer a guideline. It is important not to wait for complete 'failure' to develop spoken language, however, before trying alternatives. In the beginning other forms can serve as augmentative to speech, in the hope that they will aid its understanding and development, and are not necessarily alternatives to spoken language.

Nevertheless, there is some evidence that individuals with autism find it difficult to take in information from more than one channel at the same time and this has suggested to some teachers that alternative forms of communi-cation should not be taught alongside speech, but rather separately. However, others have reported beneficial effects on the understanding and development of spoken language when an alternative accompanies speech and most practitioners find it most natural to accompany signs or symbols with speech. Early studies suggested that speech did not develop in individuals with autism through their being taught speech/sign combinations alone but only if there were additional speech training sessions. Others have claimed that speech does develop from sign training. In one longitudinal study involving ten children over a period of 18 months by one of the authors, a few of the children did begin to speak during the course of the study but there was no relationship between this and the number of signs acquired or used; some children acquired a signing vocabulary of over 300 without producing any speech at all.

CHOOSING A SYSTEM OF COMMUNICATION

Although the prime goal is communication, that can only be achieved in its fullest sense if the individual has a means with which to communicate. Clearly, most parents and educators would want the individual with autism to communicate using the spoken (and if possible, also the written) form of the language spoken by the community. This is so for the obvious reasons of ease of communication with the family and with the wider community, of easier access to all forms of education and cultural material, and because it will help the individual to integrate into that community. Thus, early goals would be to improve spoken language skills as well as teaching for and about communication. However, as we have seen, this will not be a feasible long-term goal for all.

Choosing the most appropriate system will depend to some extent on the individual and the context of the teaching. Teachers and parents (for decisions on the communication system to use must, above all else, involve a consensus view) cannot base the decision purely on the child's preferred medium (vision, for example) without taking the communicative environment into account. It would be unwise, for example, for teachers in a school to carefully devise individual communication programmes for each child solely on the basis that each child would use a language system best suited to their particular cognitive, linguistic and physical functioning. The result would be a situation in which children would not see a model of their own system being used for communication at all. The very essence of communication is that it is a shared system and, while there can be some individual variation within a class or family group, there must be a system that is understood and used by all the adult members of the communicating group at least.

THE TEACHING OF SIGN

The benefits of sign for individuals with autism have been documented, but teaching sign is not a panacea for the communication problems in autism. Increasing experience in the teaching of sign to individuals with autism has reinforced some of the benefits while also highlighting the limitations and suggesting new limitations from the way in which sign is commonly taught.

The potential benefits are:

- For some individuals who will remain mute it provides an alternative means through which they can learn to communicate.
- Signing provides a more readily comprehended means of communication which may help understanding of communication itself and of the accompanying spoken language.
- Having to use an unfamiliar language of sign may make teachers slow down their rate of accompanying spoken language and perhaps even limit it to key concepts.
- The need to consider whether or not to sign to a peer is one concrete way of getting a speaking pupil with autism to consider the listener's needs in a 'conversation'.

Yet in practice there are also disadvantages:

- When used as an 'alternative' to speech it severely limits the communication environment to those who are familiar with that particular sign language. This is a particular problem because individuals with autism who have failed to develop a spoken language seem to have almost as much difficulty in acquiring a signed one and so they are unlikely to be proficient enough to join a signing community. Nor is their own signing likely to be much understood outside the confines of the teaching environment. Even within many schools there will be only a small number who are proficient signers.
- Using sign as augmentative to speech may help with understanding that speech, and sign may make some communicative functions clearer. Yet the way sign is taught in many schools, with a generally low standard of fluency among staff, means that the pupil is seldom exposed to good models of how to use sign in real communicative situations and signing becomes another meaningless response that needs to be gone through to get what one wants.
- It is still true that lack of fluency in sign may lead to beneficial results in terms of delivery of speech and sign, but it also has deleterious consequences. Not only will staff fail to use sign for their own communicative purposes (as above) but they often fail to use sign at all (because they cannot think of the right sign) and even fail to use any accompanying 'helpful' gesture (because they have rejected the use of gestures in favour of systematic signs). The end result is then less help for the pupil in understanding speech than in a situation where there has been no sign.
- The one unequivocal benefit of signing, in enabling pupils to focus on the listener's needs, is lost in many establishments where signing is only taught to non-speaking pupils.

Our conclusion following these advantages and disadvantages is that sign should continue to be taught to all the pupils in the school but allied to a pictorial system whose meaning is clear to naïve others and to the pupil her or himself (symbol cards may serve this purpose for many, but others may need direct photographs of the items). Sign should be taught in its communicative context, as with any other language, and staff should attempt to use it for their own genuine communication needs. The emphasis should be on sign and/or gesture as a way of making the meaning of spoken language and communication situations clear to the pupil. Gesture should not be despised as confusing, but respected as augmentative to speech in the same way that sign is.

USING THE PUPILS' OWN RESPONSES

Most of the rhetoric concerning the education of pupils with autism stresses a 'child-centred' approach, even if this is not always the case in practice. Starting the communicative process, by imputing meaning to the child's non-communicative expressions, is also the basis of normal language and communication development. There is some research evidence showing the effectiveness of approaches, such as imitation of the child's spontaneous actions, in getting individuals with autism to pay attention to others and to modify their behaviour.

This is not only of value in starting off the communicative process in pupils who have no other means of communication and need to start from scratch, but it is a principle that could be profitably applied to more able pupils who might have some degree of language skills but are still very communicatively impaired. As will be seen in the following chapter, echolalia will have some communicative intent in the majority of cases and, far from trying to repress the child's response, we should be building on it to try to develop further communicative aspects. The same principle applies to apparently non-communicative uses of language; we should look for any communicative intent that might be there or might sensibly be imputed. If we can look at the language behaviour of pupils with autism in the light of the fundamental difficulties with communication discussed above, and also remember the problems caused by the particular educational uses of language, then we can develop approaches more geared to facilitating communication than to producing behavioural conformity.

TEACHING ABOUT COMMUNICATION

Programmes such as TEACCH[31] clarify the dimensions that need to be considered when teaching communication skills and stress the need to teach one dimension only at a time. Teaching language to individuals with autism, then, needs to move away from the old techniques of teaching a vocabulary (whether of speech or sign) and then teaching more sophisticated linguistic expressions, i.e. concentrating on teaching the forms and 'words' for communication only. The individual does need to be taught some means to communicate with, but the more fundamental teaching priority is to teach about communication. Most specialist teaching, at least, does pay attention to the dimension of context as well as that of form and vocabulary in that it takes account of the fact that being taught something in one context does not mean that the pupil with autism will have that skill in another situation or with another person. Programmes cope with this either by teaching in the functional context where the behaviour will be used, or by specifically teaching generalisation of the skill.

Thus form, vocabulary and context are usually taught, but what of the other two dimensions: semantic and communicative functions? Most teachers find it very difficult to separate these two dimensions conceptually and in practice it is not essential to do so. Thus we are really talking only about one missing dimension but it is the one that defines the difficulty in autism, that is, the one concerned with communication itself. The reason this dimension is often neglected in teaching may be that it is so much a natural part of normal social situations that it is difficult to isolate it as a dimension, and even more difficult to think about teaching it.

Another important teaching point to remember is that the teaching is unlikely to be successful if more than one dimension is taught at a time. This can be neglected as a factor, especially when one of the dimensions is communicative function which comes so naturally to most of us. For example, a boy may be able to ask for an apple readily in a variety of contexts, displaying ability in vocabulary (knowing the word for apple), form (saying the word), context (with different people on different occasions in different places) and function (making a request). This boy likes apples and has learnt to ask for them with comparative ease. Encouraged by this, the teacher sees pears in the fruit bowl and decides to try to teach him to say 'pear', but this time there is tremendous difficulty and no success after weeks of trying. What is going wrong?

On the face of it, learning to say 'pear' does not seem that different from learning to say 'apple'. However, the boy does not like pears and so when he is being asked to say 'pear' he is being asked not to use a communicative function of 'request' (as was the case with the apple) but to use one of 'comment'. As we have already noted 'comment' is inherently more difficult a function for individuals with autism to understand than 'request', but that is not the main problem. The real stumbling block for him is that he is being asked to learn two things at the same time—to learn a new vocabulary item ('pear') and a new communicative function ('to comment').

A better teaching programme, with more chance of success, is first to teach the new communicative function of 'comment', while keeping everything else the same. Thus, the boy would be taught to say 'apple' when he had just eaten one (or more than one if there is the likelihood that he would want to eat more than one at a sitting) and presumably did not want another at that point. The teacher might assume that there would be no teaching involved since he can already say 'apple', but this time he would be being asked to use it to comment on an apple in the bowl, or in a tree, or a picture of an apple in a book, and the teacher may well find that he cannot automatically apply the use of 'apple', as a request, to its use as a comment. Only when the boy has been able to show that he understands 'apple' used as a comment, and can use it in that way himself, should he be asked to learn new words (like 'pear') to use in this way.

TEACHING COMMUNICATIVE FUNCTIONS

The easiest communicative function to start with is that of request, for this can most readily be demonstrated and, as we have seen, it is the first (and sometimes the only) communicative function to develop in autism. But even here there is sometimes a failure to appreciate the problem. Take a common situation in the school day, a period when staff and pupils sit round a table for a drink and perhaps a biscuit or (in more healthy places) a piece of fruit. The pupils are commonly required to ask for what they want in some appropriate manner (pointing, speaking, signing) before being given it. Of course, there is nothing wrong with this procedure as such, but are the pupils learning about communication? Well, they are learning some relevant communication skills—practising the correct vocabulary items, using as advanced a form of communication as they are able (the teacher will not usually accept a point, if the pupil is capable of using speech or a sign to indicate choice, for example) and using a form that is functional in that context (it achieves the required result). But this procedure does not really help the pupils discover what communication is about.

What the pupils learn in that situation is a particular routine tied to a particular context and some will not even realise that communication is occurring; they may sign under the table, whisper their request inaudibly or 'talk to the wall' without securing an audience. And, if they want the snack, what is the commonest 'mistake' they make? They reach out to take the snack without asking. As with most errors, this is the greatest clue to what they are really learning. The situation is obviously one where there is no true need to communicate; they can just take what they want. By preventing them from doing this and teaching a preliminary 'ritual' that must be gone through first, the teacher does not teach about communication but about conformity, politeness, waiting turns and so on. These are all useful skills but not directly related to what communication is about. To do this, the teacher must ensure that the children need to communicate their requests by maintaining obvious control over the snacks.

We have already noted that to teach about communication in a request situation, the pupils' only way of obtaining what they want must be through somebody else. In a similar way the teacher will need to create a communicative need in order to teach any of the communicative functions, and this gets more difficult the more the functions deal with influencing another's mental states rather than just their actions. 'Comment' is an example of a function that can be successfully taught using the pupil's interests (the principle of starting where the child is and using spontaneous behaviour to try to invoke communicative intent). This may be done by shutting a favourite item (in full view of the child) in one of a series of containers 'labelled' in a particular way, for example, with a picture of something the pupil knows but is not particularly involved with. The pupil, in asking for his or her item, then, has to indicate which container it is in, by giving the appropriate label. This is then repeated for a number of different kinds of containers, but always with the correct one having the same label. In time this label comes to have significance for the pupil but still does not represent an object that the pupil wants. Thus, when the pupil notices the label (introduced into a picture book perhaps), and, we hope, draws attention to it by labelling it, the pupil is making a comment and not a request.

DISRUPTIVE BEHAVIOUR AS COMMUNICATION

One of the most useful ways of looking at disruptive behaviour is to treat it 'as if' it were communication and to try to work out what communicative function the behaviour is serving. Further details on this are given in the chapter on behaviour management.

A COMPENSATORY VERSUS A REMEDIAL COMMUNICATION CURRICULUM

Once we begin to unpick the myriad skills needed to learn to communicate, it all seems a hopeless task. This is especially so when, as in most cases, the pupil may never really understand the nature of communication and will just come to apply a set of learnt routines, albeit in a more flexible and useful way. Some educationists feel that since this is the reality and teaching time is short, the pupil should be taught specific compensatory skills only. Thus, rather than trying to improve understanding of communication itself, the teacher should concentrate on teaching the pupil to express choices and to understand enough to function in as independent a way as possible. As an example of this, the TEACCH[32] programme uses pictorial symbols for non-verbal children, for the communication of needs only. These symbols are readily understood by untrained members of the public and it gives individuals an effective way of making their needs known and thus of improving the quality of their lives. TEACCH is an example of this compensatory approach in one of its most successful forms but it does not claim to be helping the individual to any greater understanding of the communicative process itself.

For many parents and teachers this is not enough. They want to remediate the individual's difficulty with communication itself. Some are attempting to do this through educational means by, for example, trying to teach about intentions. The metacognitive approach we suggest in this book encourages individuals to become more aware of their own mental states and by analogy to come to understand those of others; it is hoped that this might then lead to some understanding of key communicative concepts such as 'joint attention' and 'shared knowledge'.

None of the remedial approaches has yet shown unequivocal success and in the meantime most schools aim to incorporate both remedial and compensatory approaches into the curriculum. Teaching communication is a difficult task which is more easily tackled in informal situations rather than a traditional school setting and it is one with which most teachers feel inadequately equipped to deal. And yet it is the most crucial aspect of educating pupils with autism. It is another example in the education of pupils with autism where close co-operation with parents is essential. It is easier to emphasise the communicative uses of language, for example, in informal settings than it is in an educational setting where language has more academic purposes and the needs of other pupils must be considered (this being especially problematic in integrated settings).

CONCLUSION

Communication is at the core of the autistic difficulty with learning and it must therefore be at the heart of any effective educational approach with pupils with autism. The nature of the problem means that there are no easy solutions, but there are optimistic ways forward. We have tried to show in this chapter why it is so important to take on the intellectual challenge of what to do about communication before focusing on particular strategies related to language.

The Development of Language

5

THE RANGE OF LANGUAGE COMPETENCE

It is communication rather than language difficulties that are characteristic of autism in spite of the very obvious abnormalities and delays in the development of language that are often present. Because autism is a biological disorder affecting brain function, it is likely that whatever has led to the autism may have caused additional disturbance to brain function, and 'pure' autism, without additional developmental problems, will only be present in a minority of cases. Many individuals with autism, therefore, will have additional problems which lead to further language difficulties. Severe learning difficulties or associated specific language difficulties often mean that general language development is severely delayed and in a significant minority of cases the individual remains mute.

This may be because of specific language difficulties which mean the child has no natural inborn mechanism for learning the structure of language. It is known that autism is associated genetically with language disorder and that there are often language difficulties in family members of individuals with autism. But this association is not there in every case and some individuals with autism have an ability to acquire the structural aspects of language as a special 'islet of ability' (which may extend to foreign languages).

More commonly, however, there are difficulties in acquiring language which extend to all its forms, including sign, as we have seen. Spoken language ability in autism ranges from muteness to an apparent facility. Where language is acquired, a facility with the structure and form may mislead the naïve listener into a false sense of the individual's comprehension. It is usual to assume that understanding precedes production but this is not necessarily the case in autism where, even though speech has good structural form and may be prolific, an analysis will show that the individual's understanding of the language may be well below his or her ability to produce it. Speech in autism will tend to be non-productive, often showing both immediate and delayed echolalia. It will also tend to be pedantic and uttered in a monotone or with unusual intonation and stress. Reading may be easier than telling a simple story or relating a past event coherently.

PROBLEMS WITH THE LANGUAGE OF TEACHING AND LEARNING

LANGUAGE BEFORE COMMUNICATION

The pupil with autism will have problems in the educational uses of language, which build on the assumption that communicative uses have already been firmly established in the pre-school years. It is only in autism that children may acquire language and then have to learn the communicative uses for it. The child with autism will not understand about communication and so will have little idea of what language is for. Effective communication, as we have seen, requires paying attention to what the speaker intends but this is liable to be lost on the child with autism. As a corollary to this, the teacher will be unprepared for the child's interpretations and thus will make interpretations of the child's responses that do not allow for the child's lack of communicative understanding.

Even in specialist settings for those with autism, it is difficult to maintain this constant awareness of what to us is such an alien interpretation, as the following incident illustrates. The school were in the middle of a project on sheep and this particular assembly was about wool. The teacher leading the assembly held up a fleece and asked: 'Does anyone know what this is called?' Hands were raised and the teacher chose one boy from his class where this topic had been well covered and who seemed eager to respond. 'Yes,' said the boy, 'I do.' and sat down again. The teacher realised his mistake (that the child had interpreted the question literally) but in his attempt to retrieve the situation fell into exactly the same trap. 'It's called a fleece', he said, and added, turning to the boy who had just answered so literally, 'Do you know why it is called a fleece, John?' 'Yes', said John happily, and promptly sat down. Since this was a specialist school, the teacher at least realised that it was he who had made the same mistake twice and did not, as might well have happened in a mainstream setting, interpret the boy's behaviour as rude or cheeky.

LITERACY AND SPOKEN LANGUAGE

There are also problems with the assumption that literacy emerges from spoken language development, since this may well not be the case in autism. Many pupils with autism will find reading and even writing easier to understand and use than spoken language and certainly reading a story may well come earlier than being able to tell one, even from a picture book without words. As we have seen, the structure of even a simple narrative may be best approached first through reading rather than trying to get the child to tell the teacher, regardless of spoken language skill. Written language could be easier to understand than spoken language since it is more static and changes less with intonation and voice quality. Children with autism, then, may learn to read and write without ever learning to speak, or as a precursor to it, and may read beyond their level of understanding (hyperlexia). No assumptions can be made, therefore, about a particular relationship between the ability to read and the ability to understand and use spoken language.

CLASSROOM LANGUAGE

It is not only the way that language is used in the classroom that causes difficulty, however, but the kind of language that is used. Educational language moves away from the here and now and begins to talk about things beyond children's immediate and personal understandings, introducing abstract concepts with abstract language. Teachers are also likely to introduce new concepts by using metaphors on the, normally valid, assumption that it is easier to understand something new if it is explained in terms of something familiar. Now it is possible to understand a simile (that something is like something else) through a literal interpretation of the words and, providing they have sufficient language ability, this will present no problems for children with autism. But metaphors require an understanding of mental states, in that the listener has to divorce the image of the *real* object (as would be expressed by the literal use of the word) from its mental image (as evoked by the metaphor). As we have seen, this is very difficult for children with autism to grasp. Thus, we would expect them to be happy with expressions such as 'I want you all to be as quiet as mice' but completely at a loss if this is expressed as 'I want you all to be little mice'.

Even more difficult for children with autism are those expressions used in classrooms that rely not only on understanding mental states but also on being aware of an attitude to that mental state (a second order mental state). This is what is involved in irony or sarcasm where the listener has to understand that what is said may be contrary to the literal meaning and is *deliberately* so, thus revealing the speaker's true feelings. Even the most able pupils with autism may puzzle over such uses of language.

For example, a young man with autism, now in his twenties, recently met his support teacher from 12 years previously and greeted her with, 'When you said "Thank you very much!" you were being sarcastic'. The teacher knew he had been having lessons in understanding sarcasm for a number of years, so she guessed the context of his utterance, but could not remember the incident to which it referred. The young man, of course, could, and reminded her of an incident where they had been sharing a table on which all her files were spread out. As the session finished, the boy (then 12) got up rather clumsily and knocked the files onto the floor. The teacher, without thinking, said sarcastically 'Thank you very much!' The boy had not queried this at the time and the teacher had clearly forgotten it, but it had been a source of bewilderment to him which he had only been able to resolve years later following specific teaching. This illustrates the unconscious stress and confusion a teacher can cause by unthinking use of language, but also shows the incredible tenacity which many individuals with autism will display in trying to resolve their own difficulties.

LANGUAGE AS AN ADDED CONFUSION

For the less able pupil with autism, or those with additional language difficulties, the mere use of language as a mode of instruction can be a source of difficulty. Teachers should therefore look at the use of alternative or at least augmentative forms of instruction wherever possible. The majority of pupils with autism learn more effectively without additional verbal explanation or direction. The ideal situation seems to be where there is enough visual and/or kinaesthetic and haptic (from the movements involved and the feel of the task materials) information in the presentation of the task for the child with autism to be able to understand immediately how to tackle the task and when it is complete.

Because of their own verbal ways of learning, teachers might have their own preferences that cause them to talk their pupils through tasks, even where such talk is superfluous. Also, it may seem somehow demeaning, for example, to manipulate a child through tying his or her shoelaces without a running commentary on the lines of, 'We just put this like this dear, and then, see that little hole? We're just going to put this loop . . . '. It seems as if talking in this way is part of expressing a caring attitude and recognising the other's humanity and we feel uncomfortable in not doing so. We are diffident, therefore, in suggesting a course of action that may lead to a less caring attitude to those with autism, and all we would suggest is that teachers and carers be aware that language is more often a source of confusion than help and that, even where it is used, it should be backed with supporting information from other sources.

CLASSROOM DISCOURSE AS A MODEL

It should be remembered that classrooms are social situations in their own right with their own form of culture. Part of that culture is a particular style of discourse, appropriate to that setting. Classroom discourse styles may be hard for the pupil with autism to learn but, in fact, they may be acquired more readily than freer conversational modes. This carries the danger that pupils with autism might adopt this rigid form for informal situations also—taking, for example, the 'teacher' style of adherence to a single topic regardless of addressees' interests or responses, asking questions when the answer is already known, and so on. Clearly this is not a model discourse style for someone who has not already mastered the interdependent nature of most natural conversations. It is not generally feasible to alter the style of classroom discourse entirely, but teachers should be aware of this danger and provide other times for, and specific teaching of, more informal styles. They will also need to ensure that the different styles are clearly 'marked' for the pupils with autism and that they understand the appropriateness of each to different contexts.

TEACHING LANGUAGE

The 1960s and 1970s saw the growth of behavioural methods in all aspects of education for those with special educational needs. This included the teaching of language and many programmes were introduced to teach both pre-linguistic and linguistic skills. These were taught in one-to-one sessions out of context and using extrinsic and often non-functional rewards. But dissatisfaction soon developed with these methods, especially for language teaching, when the results were seen to lack generalisation and not to lead to any spontaneous skill.

The usual argument for a more natural approach is that such an approach utilises the natural ability of all children to acquire language. The counter argument is that where there is a specific language impairment there is no natural language learning ability to tap into, and in the case of autism there is no foundation of communication skills which can act as a 'bootstrap' for learning language in a natural way. The problem with autism is that, while this is true for natural language learning, it is also true for teaching language in a more directive way. Just as the more able children with autism may acquire the structural aspects of language but fail to understand the pragmatic aspects of how language is used in its social context, so it may be possible to teach the formal structural aspects of language but with equal lack of success in teaching pragmatic understanding.

It may be that one-to-one sessions with a language therapist will be very effective for some aspects of language learning. Assessment of the formal aspects of language, for example, is best carried out in this way and this kind of individual teaching may also be necessary for initial vocabulary learning, to help understanding of particular language forms, or for building up communication skills with one other person. Even so, such teaching should have a functional and communicative bias. If language is taught in a rigidly behavioural way, divorced from its communicative context, then this will make it difficult for pupils with autism to learn about language in its social context. Learning will be sterile unless children are taught the social meaning of what they have learnt and how and when to use those forms for communication.

To illustrate this difference, consider the case where the teacher wants the pupil to learn colour names. A behavioural approach to this might be to show a colour, verbally prompt its name and reward the child (perhaps with a piece of chocolate) for repetition of the correct name. Subsequently, the prompts would be gradually faded until the child was being rewarded for giving the name when shown the colour. There would then be a programme of 'overlearning' when the child would be given lots of practice at naming the colour while the rewards were reduced. Finally, the response would be generalised by rewarding responses to that colour in other situations, for other objects, with other people and to a gradually increasing colour range that would normally be classified as the same colour. This might well be successful in enabling the child to name that colour, but it has done nothing to explain the communicative aspects of such naming. Children with autism who have been taught language forms in such a mechanistic way often display their lack of understanding of the pragmatic aspects by using them inappropriately, blurting out the name of the colour whenever it is seen, for example, regardless of the appropriateness of doing so.

There needs to be a way of teaching, in this example, colour names, that takes account of the child's difficulties with understanding when, how and to whom to use the terms (the pragmatics). The first step is to get the child to name the colour in a context where there is some communicative purpose in doing so. The teacher could place some favourite item of the child's in one of several identical containers distinguished from the others only by that particular colour painted on its side. The containers should be in such a position that the child needs to ask the teacher to obtain access to them. If the child then indicates in some way (perhaps by naming the object, pointing at the container or throwing the teacher's hand towards it) that he or she wants the hidden object, the teacher will say 'Where is your x [the object in question]? Oh! It's in the y [the colour being taught] box. Do you want me to open the y box? Say "y"'. The child is still being prompted to say the name and will still get rewarded for saying it, but this time there is a communicative link between the child saying the colour and being given the reward; that is, there is a reason for naming the colour of the box which makes sense in a communicative context. The familiar techniques of the behavioural programme may, then, only need minor adaptations to fit a curriculum which takes account of the communicative difficulties of the child.

LITERACY AND AUTISM

A written instruction can be taken in at the pupil's own rate and remains available for consultation. This gives it advantages over spoken instructions which may require a division of attention between task and instruction, may be confused by the social signals accompanying their delivery, and will require a capacity to memorise and retrieve at will. Written instructions are also likely to be more explicit, making fewer assumptions about the child's understanding of what the speaker intends.

Nevertheless, literacy skills are not automatically better than spoken language skills in autism and there has been some recent research linking Asperger's syndrome with dyslexia. Since dyslexia is a form of language impairment and autism is linked with language difficulties, it would not be surprising to find some pupils with autism who also have dyslexia. This would be particularly likely in Asperger's syndrome where some research suggests a general motor clumsiness in early development (unlike the good motor development that is generally characteristic of autism) linked to later problems with articulation. Many, if not all, children with dyslexia would share this developmental history.

In terms of academic skills, dyslexia may be as great a barrier to learning as autism, especially in a mainstream context, and so these needs should not be neglected simply because they are additional to the autism. The kinds of structured approaches to literacy that are usually recommended for pupils with dyslexia, will, in any case, provide a good foundation for teaching pupils with autism and be appropriate to the autistic style of learning. Thus, teaching pupils with dyslexia to operate a word processor through the use of proper keyboard skills (rather than permitting the typical two- or three-finger typing) has been shown to enhance spelling and reading ability by providing a motor memory (through the pattern of finger positions) for each word. It is likely that such an approach would also be helpful to those with autism, whether or not they had additional dyslexia. Also, children with dyslexia and those with autism would benefit from learning to read and write with cursive script rather than being laboriously taught print which will need 'unlearning' when the child is taught a cursive script at a later age.

SPECIFIC LANGUAGE PROBLEMS

PRONOUN 'REVERSAL'

There is a well-documented difficulty with speaker–addressee pronouns in autism ('I'/'me'/'you'). The term 'pronoun reversal' is really a misnomer since it is very rare for the child to actually reverse the use of these pronouns. More commonly, children with autism will not use the first person pronoun but will refer to themselves as 'you' or even with the use of the third person pronoun ('he' or 'she'), presumably because these are the terms that are used to, or about, the child that the child has learnt. Because of the confusion, adults will often use proper names instead of pronouns (as they would with young normally developing children) and so many children with autism come to adopt this strategy both in self reference and to refer to others.

Research by one of the authors has shown that the problem is not due to lack of differentiation between self and other since individuals recognise and can use proper names with correct reference.[12] Rather, the difficulty lies in the way in which reference is determined in pronominal expressions. 'I' and 'you', for example, refer not to individuals but to roles within a conversational structure. 'I' is largely redundant in understanding what the speaker means, serving a purely indexical function of 'the one who is speaking'. Children with autism will have little understanding of the need to indicate conversational roles and thus are unlikely to use 'I' until they learn to do so as a rote form. Since they are also severely delayed in engaging in the kinds of pretend play in which social roles are taken, they will have less opportunity to use and practise such forms as part of imitated speech patterns, pretending to be daddy in the home corner, for example.

Some of the difficulty and delay in using 'I' may, however, come from the difficulty in establishing a sense of an experiencing self. Children begin to use 'I' around the age when they are becoming self-assertive and developing a strong sense of self-agency so that phrases such as 'I do it!' are amongst the earliest uses. The child also needs to understand about conversational roles before learning the labels for them. Otherwise, the child merely learns the label as a 'name' for a person rather than a role, and this leads to the characteristic confusions. Merely correcting the terms used without increasing the child's understanding will not be very effective.

The confusion over 'you' is more profound and more clearly related to difficulty in understanding mental states. 'You' refers to the addressee but it may not be an addressee who is physically present. The only way of establishing the real reference for 'you' is to appreciate who the speaker intends to be the addressee of his or her remarks. Explicit teaching of the reference for 'you', in a contrived situation where there are two adults to model the role of speaker–addressee pronouns, can help individuals with autism resolve this problem, for situations where the addressee is physically present. But pronoun assignment is likely to remain mysterious when it is the speaker's intentions only that determine reference, for example, for written prose that addresses the reader directly. Even when the addressee is present there is likely to be confusion in English if there is more than one other there; the listener must use eye gaze, body posture or pragmatic understanding of what the speaker intends, to work out if everyone is being addressed by the 'you' or which subset it refers to. All these are key areas of deficit in autism and so it is not surprising that there is extreme delay in understanding the reference for 'you'. There may be some clues to reference in languages that have a plural and singular form for this addressee pronoun but then there is additional confusion when usage of these forms obeys politeness rules rather than rules of number.

Although there is absolutely no evidence to support a psychodynamic view of the aetiology of autism, or confusion over a sense of self, the sense of self is nevertheless crucial in the use of the first person pronoun. This pronoun only refers to the self as a conversational role, or an experienced agent of action ('I') or recipient of action ('me'). Individuals with autism will have little understanding of conversational role and, without an experiencing sense of self, may not express this agent or recipient role either. Thus, general work within a cognitive curriculum, that can help the individual build up a sense of themselves performing actions, will help in the acquisition of this pronoun.

In a more direct way, the child can be taught to label his or her own assertive acts, using the 'I' pronoun, even if this is only in imitation at first. It is often in the imitative use of 'I', while taking on adult roles in symbolic play, that the young normally developing child first comes to use this pronoun. Similarly, 'me' can be taught directly in the course of everyday social exchanges. Care should be taken, however, that 'me' is taught alone, because the child cannot be relied upon to understand the correct referential breaking points in speech. Thus, a girl of ten with autism and severe learning difficulties was taught to use 'me' to refer to herself instead of referring to herself by name, in the context of receiving a drink. She was taught to respond to the question 'Who would like a drink?' with the polite phrase 'Me, please'. Unfortunately, she had little understanding of the process and ten years later still refers to herself as 'me please', which is more confusing and bizarre than if she were still using her own name as self reference.

It has been shown that normally developing children resolve the dilemma of the reference for 'you' (which they commonly first take to be another name for themselves, since this is the most salient use of 'you' that they hear) when they observe others being referred to with this label. Children with autism do not observe the conversations of others in this interested fashion and so do not expose themselves to this learning. It is up to the teacher, therefore, to contrive situations in which others, as well as the child, are addressed as 'you' and in which the child is rewarded for recognising correctly the reference for you in each case. Experiments attempting to teach pronoun resolution in this way with children with autism have shown that the more able can learn if they are given these very structured and specific lessons, but that those with severe learning difficulties and language disorder or delay, are not able to master pronoun use in this way.[24] In such cases it may be better to allow the use of names instead of pronouns to avoid confusion.

REPETITIVE QUESTIONING

The function of questions in conversations is another area where full understanding cannot be reached unless the listener takes account of the speaker's intentions and the social context that gives the clues to this. Few questions are purely 'sincere' questions, where speakers want information that they believe addressees possess. In educational contexts, questions are often 'display' questions where the teacher wants to know what the pupil knows and to judge the knowledge against his or her own. If children with autism do not have a background understanding, because they have not engaged in communicative exchanges, they may become very confused by the educational model of question use presented in schools.

Other questions may be rhetorical in one of two ways. One is where the speaker assumes that the addressee not only knows the answer but knows that the speaker and everyone else knows the answer as well. Examples of such questions are 'Is rain wet?' or 'Who wants a life like that?' Here the intention of the speaker is an assertion not a request for information. It is a comment expressing an attitude about what has gone before. Thus, if someone is asked if they want to go on holiday, for example, and they respond with the rhetorical question 'Is rain wet?', that can only be understood as an answer to the first question if it is clear that everyone, including the speaker, already knows that rain is wet. Similarly, if someone is maintaining that it is possible to live on a very low income if one never goes out or has any luxuries and someone else says, 'Yes, but who wants a life like that?' then that comment only retains its meaning if it is assumed by everybody that the answer (namely, 'nobody') is accepted by everybody.

The other kind of rhetorical question assumes that neither the addressee nor anyone else knows the answer. Questions such as 'Why is life so unfair?' or 'How did you get to be so beautiful?' lose their point if the addressee starts to give them a genuine answer. They depend for their meaning on the fact that they are unanswerable. Again, the listener has to use pragmatic knowledge, about what the speaker intends, to recognise these as assertions and not as requests for information.

A common alternative to the information-seeking function for questions is the question used to seek reassurance. The questions used for this purpose will require the same answer in order to be reassuring. Thus, 'Do you love me?' said a thousand times is still looking for the answer 'Yes' and if the lover turns round and says 'I'm not answering that any more. You know the answer' the questioner is more likely to assume that the answer is 'no' than 'yes'. The greater the need for reassurance, the more likely it is that the question will be asked and the least likely is it that a suggestion that they already know the answer will be accepted. Similarly, questions may be used to express anxiety and these are also often repeated as in the anxious 'What's the time now?' said every few seconds as we are stuck in a traffic jam on the way to an important meeting. Again, it does little to resolve our anxiety if our companion simply lists the changing times at each 30-second question or refuses to answer. What we are looking for is an acknowledgement of the real purpose of our questions and some reassurance about the fact that there is still time to get there or how the effects of being late can be minimised.

It is not surprising that individuals with autism find it difficult to answer and use questions appropriately since they will have no idea of the intentions of others (or even that they have intentions) and no idea of how to affect the mental states of others. Thus questions, when used, tend to be directed at eliciting a particular behaviour (either a motor or verbal action, or both). For example, they may always demand the same answer to repetitive questions and may persist in asking the same question until the 'correct' response is given. When it comes to answering questions, individuals with autism seem to favour a literal interpretation, taking account of what the words mean but not of what the speaker intends.

Rather than trying to stop repetitive questioning, for example, we can use it to find out what the pupil knows about questions and then teach other ways of obtaining the same communicative ends and show how other communicative ends can be achieved by the same form, i.e. questions.

As an example take the case of a pupil who asks repetitively about something he has already been told: that he is not going to have a cookery lesson today because the teacher is ill. He dreads cookery lessons because he has to give up the pads he likes to hold in his hands to stop himself self-mutilating. The teacher may wonder why he keeps asking 'Am I going to have cooking today with Louise?' Being told, 'You already know the answer to that because you've been told' is not very helpful because this takes the 'normal, sincere' question purpose (that you ask questions to find out information) as being the pupil's purpose in asking the question. Almost certainly this is not the case. The pupil is unlikely to think that the teacher has information that he does not have, since he does not think of anyone's mental state as separate to his own. A more likely explanation for the pupil's behaviour is that this is something he feels anxious about and wants to raise with the teacher so that he can be reassured by the answer again; he knows what the teacher is going to say, his purpose in asking is to get her to say it. Of course this is just the model of the use of questions that he is exposed to daily in the teacher's asking of 'display' questions.

A more helpful response on the part of the teacher, then, would be to acknowledge the pupil's communicative intent and to give him an alternative way of expressing it, e.g. 'I know cookery lessons worry you so you want to hear me tell you that there is no cookery today don't you? Don't worry! You are right. There is no cookery, but instead of keeping on asking me the same question, why don't you tell me about how you feel? You could tell me that you are glad that there is no cooking today because you don't like cooking, for example.' The teacher could then go on (or take the opportunity on another occasion, perhaps at a more suitable time) to teach another use for questions other than getting a predicted response. If the teacher wanted to continue with the topic to show the pupil how it could be extended appropriately, she could get him to ask another question to which he did not know the answer. Thus, 'If you want to find out when Louise is coming back you could ask me that question', and if this is done successfully, 'Is there something else you want to know about Louise or what you are doing today that you do not know already, that you would like to ask me?' Of course all this appears rather artificial but then teaching communication skills explicitly is bound to seem rather unnatural, because it is.

Sometimes repetitive questions are not about topics of anxiety but are ways of introducing the speaker's own obsessional topic. There are two issues to tackle here. One is to give the individual another way of introducing the topic he or she wants to discuss. This will involve teaching ways of introducing, maintaining and changing topics by the use of polite topic shifters such as, 'That is very interesting; that reminds me of x', where x is the desired topic. This is a very skilled and subtle skill to master and it is rare that individuals with autism are able to perform topic changes without abrupt or unnatural shifts in the topic. The other issue is whether, or to what extent, the individual with autism is to be allowed to talk about an obsessional topic. In such cases, artificial time limits ('you can talk about x for five minutes only, marked by this timer') or setting restrictions ('you can only talk about trains at the model train society') may have to be imposed because the individual is unlikely to be able to notice, monitor and react to appropriately, any signs of boredom or irritation in the listener.

The answer to repetitive questioning lies not in behavioural management, then, although that may be necessary as a short-term measure, but in trying to unpick the communicative intent (real or imputed) and responding to that.

LITERAL UNDERSTANDING

A characteristic of the use and understanding of language by individuals with autism is that they pay attention to the literal meaning of what is said (what the words and phrases mean) rather than to what the speaker intends to say. This is not surprising, given the kinds of difficulties noted above with understanding about intentions, but it is a complete reversal of the way normally developing children behave. Individuals with autism do not make allowances for the speaker's intentions and in that way they behave like a computer that will obey instructions to the letter even if the instruction will wipe out several days of work. Modern computer systems now make allowances for this failure to impute meaning, by getting the program to check the intentions of the user at key points and by making the consequences of particular actions explicit. This is what is needed when working with individuals with autism, but we seldom think to provide it.

There are several consequences that flow from this difficulty. One is the failure to understand polite or conventional modes of expression, and instead to take a literal interpretation. Thus, if the teacher says 'Would you like to get on with your work now Michael instead of chatting', Michael is likely to say 'No'. This may be interpreted by the teacher as extreme rudeness and disobedience of the implied command, whereas Michael has innocently and honestly responded to the question he was asked without even registering the implication. The same difficulty is apparent in understanding idiomatic expressions such as 'crying your eyes out' which can make individuals with autism fearful that their eyes will fall out when they cry.

This literal interpretation and failure to take account of the speaker's intentions can lead to problems in interpreting instructions or dealing with ambiguity. Inexperienced teachers of pupils with autism will often have had the experience of sending the child, for example, to take the register to the school office only to have the child return several minutes later still clutching the register. When the teacher then says rather crossly, 'I thought I told you to take the register to the office', the child is bewildered, because that is just what he or she has done. What the teacher did not say was to leave the register in the office and to come back without it, because the teacher assumed such instruction would be superfluous. The teacher relied on the child realising what was meant, in spite of what was or was not said, in that it would be most unlikely that the teacher wanted the child to take the register for a walk. But this kind of common-sense knowledge seems to be the most difficult for individuals with autism to acquire, since it relies on understanding motivations and intentions.

In conversations, a failure to appreciate what others can be expected to know will lead individuals with autism into characteristic discourse styles. On the one hand they may assume no shared knowledge and thus give all the information they wish to convey in explicit detail, producing a very boring pedantic style. This effect is increased by their lack of awareness of listener signals of boredom such as loss of eye contact, yawning, or attempts to interrupt or shorten the exchange. Indeed, it is often the case that if the listener is successful in interrupting the speaker with autism in an attempt to shorten the monologue, individuals with autism may go back to the 'beginning' and reiterate everything that has been said before, once they have regained the floor.

At the other extreme are individuals with autism who assume knowledge in their listeners equivalent to their own and so produce uninterpretable or ambiguous utterances where no joint reference or shared knowledge has been established. Typically, such speakers will use pronouns without establishing an unambiguous reference for them either in what they have said or in the context. For example, they may say things like 'He did it' with no indication of who 'he', or what 'it', is. They will be equally unable to monitor and recognise their listeners' responses to their speech and so they will be unaware of communication failure and will make no attempt to 'repair' the conversation to make it more explicit. Even where the listeners are themselves explicit about their lack of understanding, saying such things as 'I don't know what you mean. Who did it? What did they do?', the individual with autism may be at a loss to know how to rephrase the information to make the communication effective.

Teachers and parents who are with the young person with autism for long periods often learn to monitor their own speech to reduce the amount of ambiguity, make their intentions more explicit and avoid the use of idiom or figures of speech. This will help to reduce the confusion and stress on the child with autism and will make everyday communication easier to achieve. However, unless there is also specific teaching that draws the attention of the child with autism to these procedures, there will be no improvement in the general level of understanding and it will do nothing to help the child deal with the language of others that is not specially adapted in this way. Thus, the child with autism needs to be taught strategies that will increase his or her understanding.

At the most basic level, there are some individuals with autism who cannot even accept synonyms. One young girl of eight would have a severe temper tantrum if, for example, she was told to take off her 'jacket' when she entered the classroom because yesterday someone had called it an 'anorak'. Some teachers have tried to deal with problems like this by having a policy with all the school staff and the parents agreeing on the single label to be given to each item. This can work as a short-term way of reducing stress, but it is not good as a long-term strategy in that it is seldom possible to control the language of everyone the child comes into contact with (thus risking a tantrum when the poor unsuspecting visitor uses a 'wrong' word) and it does nothing to increase the child's level of understanding or tolerance for synonyms. A better solution is to do what was done in this case and that is to give the child a way of conveying the cause of his or her distress. In this case the girl had speech and was taught to 'correct' any words she was not happy with by giving the preferred version followed by ' . . . rather'. This strategy is still in use some 14 years later, and can become somewhat irritating to those around her, but it is an improvement on a temper tantrum and it has taught her to communicate the source of her distress, albeit in a very limited way.

In the same way, pupils with autism will need specific and explicit instruction on the interpretation of idioms, similes, metaphors, sarcasm and irony. It is only when teachers try to teach these aspects of language that they come to realise, for example, how metaphorical the English language is and thus how rich it is as a source of confusion for individuals with autism. At the most basic level of understanding, children will need to be taught that there are different ways of expressing the same meaning and this will need to be done in contexts that have salience for them. For example, in being given permission to go out to play, the child may initially only accept the first phrase that had been used for this: 'You can go out now'. Other phrases will have to be phased in gradually. One way of doing this is to reduce gradually the volume of the acceptable spoken phrase while at the same time accompanying the phrase with gestures that convey the same meaning. Eventually the spoken phrase is reduced to a whisper, then mouthed and finally disappears altogether and the gestures now are the acceptable way of expressing permission. Then a new phrase (for example, 'It's time to go') can be introduced gradually alongside the gestures, first as a whisper and then with increasing volume as the gestures are reduced in size and eventually phased out.

There are commercially available books in English that help to explain the meanings of different idiomatic and metaphorical phrases. They often give an illustration of the literal meaning of the phrase, meant to show the absurdity of that interpretation, while explaining how the phrase is normally used and what it means. Children with autism may need help to perceive the absurdity of the literal translation of the phrase and teaching is best concentrated on what the phrase *does* mean rather than on what it does not. Understanding about similes is best tackled through physical features first such as colours. Most children with autism will accept that a yellow object, for example, can be said to be 'like a buttercup' or 'like the sun' but will need more help to see how someone can be 'sunny' when the reference is not to physical characteristics but to personality traits such as cheerfulness. In some ways it may be better to teach the direct metaphorical meaning in such cases (that is, when you say 'sunny' of a person it means they are cheerful) rather than to try to teach it as a metaphor of sunshine.

When it comes to teaching about ambiguity, there are two approaches that need to be taken. The first is to teach the child to be an active listener in the sense that the child must learn to think about his or her own interpretation of what is being said and to check that interpretation through the use of pertinent questions. This process can be started in a structured way through the use of a screen dividing the child from an adult or another child, as appropriate. Each member of the dyad has a replica of the material facing the other member on their side of the screen. The adult (or peer) then gives instructions to the child to operate upon the material in some way and the child is prompted by a second adult to query any instructions that are ambiguous. For example, the child may be asked to place one of several different shapes in a container, where there are two blue shapes and thus where the instruction 'Place the blue shape in the box' would be ambiguous. If given such an instruction, the child would be prompted to see that there is a choice of two shapes and that the speaker has not given him or her enough information to decide which of the two is meant. The child is then prompted further to ask a disambiguating question which in this case would be 'Do you mean the blue square or the blue circle?'

Once the child has shown signs of understanding about ambiguity and can ask appropriate questions spontaneously (and this is likely to take a long time to achieve, if it is ever fully achieved), then the roles are switched so that the child with autism becomes the one issuing the instructions and there is then a direct check on the child's ability to give unambiguous directions, from the disambiguating questions of the adult. In this way the second aspect of learning about ambiguity—learning to give unambiguous directions—can be taught directly. There will still need to be direct teaching of these skills in everyday communicative situations to ensure generalisation.

Learning to be less pedantic, as well as less ambiguous, involves learning about shared information and that information can be withheld by oneself or others. Games can be devised that aim to teach these concepts, albeit in a very basic way, and then the child can be helped to generalise to more complex linguistic modes of expressing and withholding information. One example of such a game is 'Kim's Game' and is meant to be a test of visual memory. Items are displayed in front of the participants in the game and then covered by a cloth. The person who is 'it' then puts his or her hand under the cloth and picks up an item and wraps it in the cloth in a single movement so that no one can see the item that has been taken. The other participants must deduce what has been taken by remembering what was there originally. The point of the game for teaching about shared and private information, however, lies not in the memory aspects of the game but in the role of the person who is 'it'. When he or she is 'it', the individual with autism gains direct experience of having information (what is in the cloth) and others *not* having this information. There is also the chance to learn how information may be gained not just from what is seen or what one is told but also from logical deductions based on memory.

SPONTANEOUS SPEECH AND CONVERSATIONAL SKILLS

Conversation requires spontaneity not only in the production of utterances but in establishing the mental models of the discourse that will enable the individual to monitor its progress and actively listen to the contributions of others in order to match his or her own utterance in terms of topic relevance, style and timing. It is not surprising, therefore, that the speech of those with autism is often described as 'unproductive' and lacking in creativity while even the most able have considerable difficulty in establishing and maintaining conversations with others.

Some of the outward forms of conversational behaviour can be taught. Children can be taught to take turns by having a movable 'conch' (or a microphone attached to a PA system) to indicate each speaker's turn. They can be taught rules for entering conversations and ways of changing topic politely and even ways of closing conversations, although that is more difficult. It may even be possible to get children with autism to pay attention to what others are saying by playing games like the 'suitcase' or 'shopping trolley' game where the child has to repeat in order the items others have placed in the suitcase/trolley before adding his or her own. What is far more difficult is to teach appropriate timing for these behaviours or the very subtle responsiveness to different circumstances which is the hallmark of fluent behaviour. Videoing conversations and using them as 'micro teaching sessions', to let the individuals with autism examine their own and other people's behaviour, can be helpful, at least in dealing with some of the grosser abnormalities.

PROSODIC DIFFICULTIES

A fundamental difficulty, common to all those with autism, lies in the area of prosody. There is generally a failure to use or understand intonation as communication, in that voice quality is monotonous or follows a pattern unrelated to the meaning being conveyed. Stress is perceived but is only grasped as a focus for attention, not as a way of contrasting 'old' and 'new' information, for example. It has been suggested that these difficulties may arise from failures in the right hemisphere processing of the brain, which is generally concerned with the emotional and attitudinal aspects of speech production and comprehension. Alternatively, the difficulty may arise from the fact that processing intonation, as well as the structural and meaning aspects of language, requires simultaneous attention to two channels of information and thus there is simply information overload or an inability to attend to more than one channel at any one time. However, at a psychological level, prosodic difficulties can be seen to relate to the same kinds of communication problems as discussed previously. Intonation provides information on the speaker's attitude to what is being said and as such is a communication of that attitude. If there is no understanding of attitudes, then there will be no attempt to convey one's own or to understand others conveying theirs. This seems to fit the fact that individuals with autism can often reproduce intonation patterns exactly in their echolalic utterances yet are unable to use these intonation patterns for communicative purposes.

In a sense, there is only likely to be real improvement in this area when the individual understands about communication and therefore teaching about communication generally is the best way to help with this problem. For the more able individual with autism, however, it may be possible to give explicit instruction about the meanings that are conveyed through intonation. For example, a simple phrase such as 'I have done that!' can be said with differential stress to convey different meanings. The individual can be taught that if 'I' is stressed then the meaning is '*I* have done that as opposed to somebody else'; if the 'have' is stressed then the meaning is one of assertion that the speaker has done it in the face of someone challenging that fact; if the 'done' is stressed then the meaning is that the task has been completed in the face of someone challenging that; if the 'that' is stressed then the meaning is that the speaker has done that particular thing as opposed to something else. Such meanings can be taught in this laborious and painstaking way, but they are often difficult for even the most able individual with autism to comprehend fully and to generalise to other phrases. Nevertheless, some attempt to make intonational meanings more explicit can often prevent misunderstanding and at least makes the teacher aware of the complexities of language and communication with which the child with autism is struggling.

For the less able individuals with autism a more global approach can be used to help them become aware of the stress and intonation patterns of speech and how these relate to affectual meaning. For example, movement to music can exaggerate and emphasise these intonation patterns (stamping on the stressed word) to make them more salient. Or the pupils can express different emotions with their bodies and their voices simultaneously, for example, role-playing anger by shouting and stamping or role-playing pleasure by rocking and gently humming.

A simple game to play in one-to-one sessions with a child with autism attempts to teach the early intonational distinctions. There is an array of objects within reach of the child but not the adult. The adult points at one of these objects and makes an intonational grunt (typical of young babies) that indicates either that the object is to be handed over (a demand grunt) or that the object is to be looked at only as part of shared attention with the adult (a declarative or comment-like grunt). The child is prompted physically at first to respond appropriately to these different intonation patterns and the prompts are gradually faded until the child is able to discriminate these intonation patterns unaided. The next step is to teach the child to copy these patterns and then to attempt to play the game in reverse so that the adult responds according to the intonation pattern used by the child. Although the child does not need to be verbal to participate in this 'game', it is one that is often beneficial to the most able as well, in spite of their good structural language skills.

ECHOLALIA

Echoing what has just been said (within two conversational turns) is known as immediate echolalia whereas reproducing something overheard from longer than two turns (and the original occurrence may be from weeks or even years ago) is termed delayed echolalia. Both forms feature as part of normal language acquisition, although there is considerable individual variation in the use of echolalia as a language learning strategy. The use of echolalia in autism is notable for the length of time the strategy is used and for the particular 'parasitic' form the echolalia takes. However, there are features in the use of echolalia in autism that are common to its use in normal language acquisition and may suggest the function that it is serving.

Until recent years echolalia had been considered to be an aberrant form of behaviour described as 'self-stimulatory' and 'obsessive'. There was much energy devoted to trying to eliminate echolalia and replace it with more productive forms of communication. Different techniques employing behavioural principles or social learning theory were used, but the results were usually disappointing in terms of the results achieved and the effort expended. But recently, echolalia has been viewed in a more favourable light and it has been recognised that immediate echolalia is seldom completely non-communicative, having at least the recognition that communication consists of turns, and that delayed echolalia usually progresses along a continuum of communicativeness with or without intervention. A more effective approach, therefore, concentrates on recognising and building on the level of communication displayed in the echolalic response, and an understanding of the reasons for the echolalia will help with this process.

The situations that give rise to immediate echolalia in autism mirror those in normal language development. Where there is a failure to understand what has just been said (and it may be only one word that causes the difficulty) the individual will echo the phrase instead of responding to it. This also occurs where there is not so much a failure to understand the words but rather where there is such an overload on the individual's processing capacity (perhaps because the individual is already concentrating on something else) that he or she cannot spare the intellectual effort to process the utterance and formulate a reply. The easiest option in such circumstances is to use the language that is already 'there', in the sense that it is in short-term memory, and echo the utterance. Situations that produce echoing in individuals with autism can be altered so that the words used are known and the processing demands are less, and the echoing has then been found to give way to more productive uses of language. Similarly it has been found that in situations where individuals with autism are being pressured to speak, there is an increase in immediate echolalia whereas situations without pressure, where the interlocutor waits for spontaneous utterances, produce less overall speech from individuals with autism, but what there is is far less echolalic.

It has been suggested that some of the apparently aimless repetition of past phrases in non-communicative contexts by individuals with autism may involve a process of analysis and recombination, as in normal development, from which new phrases may emerge. What is more firmly established is that individuals with autism do begin to use apparently non-communicative phrases in increasingly communicative ways and begin to alter them to fit new communicative contexts. Thus children with autism may begin by using the echoed phrase 'Do you want a biscuit?' to indicate that they would like a biscuit themselves. To begin with they may use this to mean they want anything but later they will alter it to produce phrases such as 'Do you want a drink?' or even 'Do you want a time to go out now?'—recombining elements of two echoed phrases. In time they may even learn to change the pronoun appropriately and may produce a range of utterances whose origins in echolalia are no longer apparent.

The first step in dealing with echolalia should be an observational analysis to determine exactly how the echolalia is being used and the form it is taking. This should include analysis of the situations in which the echolalia is occurring and the linguistic form it is taking, including the way it relates linguistically to the echoed utterance. Of course, this is easier to accomplish for immediate echolalia where the 'model' utterance is directly observable. Analysis of delayed echolalia may need to infer the utterance being echoed, but it will still be possible to analyse the communicative functions being served by the echolalia and to make some deductions about the conditions that are triggering it.

The questions that need to be asked in the observational analysis, then, are:

- Is this delayed or immediate echolalia?
- Does the echoed utterance differ from the model, and if so, precisely how? (This should include some idea of whether the original intonation and accent of the speaker have been retained.)
- Is there evidence that the echoed utterance is being used to communicate something? If so, what? (At a minimum level, look for the fact that the child has recognised that there is a need to take a 'turn' in a conversation. At a more advanced level, look at whether the child persists in the echoed utterance until some end has been achieved, thus indicating the intent to achieve that purpose.)

With delayed echolalia:

- Is there evidence of change in the form being used over time?

With immediate echolalia:

- Is there evidence of failure to understand (e.g. non-compliance with an instruction)?

In a general way:

- What is the percentage of echoed to spontaneous utterances in the child's speech?

- Is this percentage increasing or decreasing?
- Are there identifiable circumstances (particular tasks, situations, settings, individuals) that provoke echolalia far more than others?

Once there is a detailed and comprehensive picture of how the child is communicating and how the use of echolalia fits into this, teaching approaches will be easier to determine. At one extreme we could have a child almost all of whose utterances are echolalic, where the echoed utterances are completely 'parasitic' in that they copy exactly the grammar, vocabulary, accent and intonation of the speaker, where there is no evidence of communicative intent beyond the recognition of 'taking a turn' in a dialogue, where echolalia is triggered by most circumstances in an unpredictable way and where this degree of echoing has continued for a number of years. It is clear that this case presents one of very little comprehension of what is being said and very little functional use. The priority in such a case would be to improve the child's understanding of spoken language, to increase the proportion of spontaneous utterances and to introduce planned variation of the echoed utterances that could be taught to the child specifically as functional ways of achieving particular communicative ends.

For example, improving understanding of spoken language would involve adopting the strategies of early child-directed speech in that the teacher would talk to the child about what he/she was doing at that moment (to ensure joint attention and ease of reference) and would do so in simplified language forms involving a lot of repetition, redundancy (talking about objects or events that were obvious to both participants in the situation) and exaggerated stress on relevant features. At the same time, the adult would introduce a lot of structured pauses for the child to 'fill' and would pause for exaggerated lengths of time for this to occur. By making incomplete sentences on a rising contour (e.g. 'Here's a lovely . . . ') instead of questions, the adult makes it easier for the child to supply the missing item. The long pauses and the slowing of interaction have also been shown to be effective in increasing the proportion of spontaneous utterances compared to echolalic ones. If the atmosphere of such sessions is relaxed, with little overt pressure on the child to speak (with the interaction continuing, supported by the adult, regardless of the contribution of the child), then this too will increase the likelihood of spontaneous utterances.

The third part of the programme for such a case would first involve imputing communicative intent to the delayed echolalic responses of the child. For example, assume that the child would say occasionally, and apparently at random (in the same intonation pattern that had been used by the teacher in the past) to no one in particular 'Time to go out to play now'. At this point, the teacher would react as if the child were using the echoed phrase as a request to go out and say 'Oh! You want to go out. Fine. Out you go!' and immediately allow the child to go out to play (at least for a while). Having reacted in this way to the child's spontaneous delayed echoing of this phrase, the teacher would then prompt the child to echo the same phrase, as immediate echolalia, when the teacher perceived that the child did want to go out. Thus, if the child was seen trying the door handle or dragging an adult to the door, the teacher would say in the same intonated phrase 'Time to go out now. You say it. Time to go out now'. The child would be given time to respond, but would be allowed out after a while, whether or not he or she responded.

Once the child had begun to echo the phrase immediately following the teacher on a regular basis, then the teacher would make the echoing of that phrase conditional on being allowed out. It is very probable that the child would soon come to utter the phrase with the communicative intent of being allowed out, without needing a direct model. Once the child was using this phrase readily with this communicative intent, the teacher would look for other situations where the child's needs were clear and where such a phrase might be adapted to fit a similar communicative intent. Thus, if the child showed signs of wanting to go to lunch, the teacher would prompt the immediate echoing of 'Time to go to lunch now' and proceed in the same way as before.

A very different set of teaching priorities would be suggested by an analysis of a child's echoing that showed much more limited and controlled echolalia. Such a child might only engage in immediate echolalia in the context of complex task instructions or when engaged in informal 'conversations' with peers and delayed echolalia might occur only when the child was alone (presumably unaware of the observer) and then with considerable variation in form. In such a case, the echoing would be much closer to that found in normal development.

Rather than concentrating on the echolalia, the emphasis here needs to be on building up language comprehension so that it does not provide an intolerable extra burden whenever tasks approach the level of the child's competency. There is also a need to develop conversational skills (e.g. introducing, maintaining and changing a topic) so that conversations can be managed without resorting to echolalia. The use of delayed echolalia to 'try out' different restructurings of phrases could be encouraged as part of normal language acquisition, albeit at a much later stage than for most children.

CONCLUSION

If a child with autism is unable to speak, teachers and carers often feel that many problems would be solved if only this barrier to communication were removed. Those who are familiar with the speaking child with autism, however, will know that the ability to speak may only make more apparent the very real and fundamental difficulties that exist with communication. Nevertheless, an ability to speak and, more importantly, to understand language is a useful asset in education and improves the prognosis for future development and quality of life. Thus, language ability should be fostered by education but teachers must also be aware that a significant minority may never achieve competence in spoken language and it is incumbent on them to ensure that a full education is received in spite of this.

The Development of Thinking

6

AUTISTIC THINKING

In this chapter we unravel the characteristics of autistic thinking and determine the implications of that particular style for learning. We lead towards the notion that what is needed for pupils with autism is a curriculum that directly addresses their specific cognitive needs. We suggest that the curriculum should be seen as a way of increasing the effectiveness of the thinking and learning style of those with autism.

This notion depends on the learner developing an awareness of him or herself as a reflecting, problem solver. Learners have to, at some level, know that they are thinking about a particular kind of problem and that it is resolvable with particular kinds of strategies which they possess. This, then, implies the development of an understanding of oneself as a person who is different from others yet who has some shared 'features' and who is capable of solving problems. And here is the root of the problem in improving thinking in autism and the starting point for any attempts to understand what can be done. Children with autism have a particular difficulty in developing an awareness of themselves and this extends to any role as 'reflective problem solver'.[25]

THE DEVELOPMENT OF AWARENESS OF SELF AND OTHERS

If we can accept that perceptual awareness of social behaviour normally fuels the development of social cognition then it is clear that problems in this area will lead to specific difficulties with mental representations (that is difficulties with understanding what others are thinking and feeling) rather than in representations in general. Our own research argues in favour of this kind of social/cognitive deficit. Indeed, psychologists have in the past tended to want to separate out thinking/feeling/understanding others (cognition/affect/social awareness), but there is a strong argument for recognising the interrelatedness of social, cognitive and emotional aspects in thinking and learning generally and suggesting that it is a breakdown within this interrelationship that causes problems in autism.

USING ONE'S OWN THINKING AS A MODEL

The difficulty that children with autism have in recognising expressions of emotion means that other people's mental states, for example, their intentions, remain obscure to them. Also, they have difficulty in using their own mental states to reflect on how others may be thinking and feeling. They do not seem able to think that because an icy cold shower is uncomfortable for them then it may well be so for someone else. Indeed, many individuals with autism do not even appear to have this level of awareness with respect to their own sensations; they experience the coldness of the shower but it is as if they do not know that they are having that experience. This is a difficult notion to grasp when for us the connection between having an experience, and knowing that we have it, is seamless and automatic.

Clearly, without the facility of being able to use one's own thinking as a model with which to interpret the thinking of others, then other aspects of thinking will also be impaired. We use the knowledge gained from our own experience of reading, for example, to set up a kind of working model in our minds of what it is like to be a reader and that enables us to have some understanding of how the reader of this book may be feeling at any point; indeed we hope that this will enable us to present our material so that it is easy to understand and interesting. As we saw in the chapters on language and communication, an inability to take the listener's (or reader's) perspective is characteristic of autism.

MEMORY PROCESSING

Lack of ability to reflect on their own thinking means that the memory processing of those with autism is qualitatively different from that of those without autism. We have already noted the paradox that children with autism often have difficulty in relating personal events and remembering the gist of narratives and yet are able to exhibit exceptional feats of rote memory. It is as if the memories are there but are not usable by the individual. Events can trigger in a child with autism whole chunks of memory recalled as complete episodes, but when asked to search memory for particular incidents that same child may have extreme difficulty. So, for example, a girl with autism might recall a particular mealtime in minute detail following cueing but be unable to remember it spontaneously when asked what she had for lunch.

To restate the memory difficulties peculiar to autism that were noted in the Introduction, the individual may be able to recall the following: autobiographical facts about themselves, episodes that do not include a personal element or that are cued, and general semantic knowledge and procedural knowledge for skills; but that same child might be unable to remember him or herself performing actions, participating in events or possessing knowledge and strategies.

In short, the memory difficulty in autism is in the development of personal episodic memory which depends on the existence of an 'experiencing self', encoding events as part of a personal dimension. A deficit in developing an 'experiencing self' would lead to a subsequent difficulty in developing personal episodic memories. In the normal pattern of development, the experiencing self enables the individual to search memory in a way that frees recall from dependence on specific cueing.

For example, a boy with autism was sent to get some scissors from the drawer. He knew where the drawer was, but when he got there the drawer was locked. He knew where the key was kept because he had been shown where it was on another occasion when he had needed paper from the same drawer. But he couldn't seem to remember where the key was now when he needed it to get the scissors. It seems that he couldn't remember himself getting the key on the other occasion because (presumably) that was not in the context of scissors, but in the context of paper. What he needed was the cue 'paper' ('go and get the key you used when you got the paper out'). Once he was given this appropriate cue he was able to remember the relevant information and successfully complete the task.

In essence, his ability to use his memory was dependent on context-specific cues. And it is the lack of an experiencing self in autism which means that the kind of memory searching that that pupil needed to do was impossible or very difficult for him, and that leads to the characteristic pattern of abilities and disabilities in autism that we have already noted.

The lack of an experiencing self has a profound effect at all stages in the processing of information. At the perceptual stage, events are experienced but in a non-subjective way. That is, individuals with autism are aware of what is happening but not aware that it is happening to them. This means they cannot truly know themselves, and the kinds of problem-solving strategies they possess and have used. Certainly, they may be able to recall when prompted but that is not the same as being able to search one's own memory in a reflective way. It leads to dependency on others and a lack of confidence or even motivation in tackling tasks, especially if they are new.

SPECIFIC COGNITIVE DIFFICULTIES IN PROBLEM SOLVING

This section discusses some of the specific difficulties that affect problem solving in autism which we have not dealt with in detail elsewhere in the book.

PERCEPTION

Another of the many paradoxes of children with autism is their inconsistent reactions to stimuli. A child may seem totally unaware of the range of sounds on one occasion and yet react to an everyday sound as if it were causing acute pain on another. A child may peer at a particular visual stimulus at one time and shy away from it as if it were hurting his/her eyes the next. This paradox extends across all the senses and includes reactions to physical pain. The reasons are not clear though it seems likely that the explanation will be at a bio-chemical level and will involve some kind of metabolic disturbance.

Whatever the reason there are knock-on effects in behavioural and psychological terms. At a behavioural level the child may 'over-react' to normal levels of stimulation and produce behaviours that indicate panic. At a psychological level there are significant implications for learning. One of the key features of the way in which we learn is our dependency on the constancy or regularity of much of our environment. Babies learn that their crying will produce someone if, and only if, their crying regularly has that result. Their learning will diminish according to the irregularity of responses to their crying. Later the child learns to read because the printed letters remain the same and the spelling of words is constant. Again, there will be a diminution in learning in direct proportion to the amount of irregularity. If the child is faced with upper case letters on one occasion and lower case the next, or if the spelling of words varies from one day to the next, then clearly learning will be impaired.

Learning is at its weakest when faced with the irregular; indeed, the usual human strategy when faced with it is to impose regularity where there may be none. If we now consider the position of children with inconsistent perceptions, we can see the pervasiveness of their difficulty, from the earliest stages of learning, where the child needs to perceive the regularity of the mother's smile, to later stages of academic learning. To try to understand the depth of the problem one only needs to try to imagine learning to name colours when their intensity changes daily.

There have been attempts to deal with perceptual abnormalities directly, mainly in the auditory field. Some therapies are based on the idea that children with autism can be taught, through a process of desensitisation, to perceive the world in a less distorted way. Miraculous cures have been claimed but the evidence is that while some children may improve it is not an answer to the underlying problem.

MOTOR DEVELOPMENT

Some children with autism also have physical difficulties which might involve problems in the execution of movements (they are clumsy) or, more commonly, involve problems in planning and intending motor movements. This kind of problem often carries a clinical diagnosis of 'dyspraxia', which may be seen either as additional to the autism or, according to some theoretical positions, as an integral part of it. Proponents of Facilitated Communication[21] as a 'cure' for autism (rather than as a useful but limited tool, which is our own view), for example, think of autism as solely a problem to do with planning and executing actions. Thus, help in performing communicative actions (through physical prompting to use the keyboard of a word processor or to point to a communication board) should suffice to eliminate the 'developmental' problems of autism, which they see as largely secondary to this primary motor problem.

We would in no way endorse this view, but we do recognise that there are some (if not all) children with autism who have problems in motor development and our account of autism, as well as our teaching, must acknowledge this and the further complications that thereby arise. Some motor problems, such as tip-toe walking, may have a neurological base, separate from the autism. Others may arise more directly from the autism itself. A lack of awareness of self may include an insecure body image and a poor idea of the location of their own body in space and thus how to move around in space. Again, this is something that develops from interactions with others and from monitoring of proprioceptive information from joints and muscles that tells us where our limbs are in relation to space; both these experiences may be limited in autism.

Even more characteristic of autism, however, are movements that directly reflect their relation to others and to the world. A poor sense of that relatedness might well lead to bodies held rigidly, rather than moulding to the person or object holding them, to difficulties in catching or throwing a ball underarm, in performing pat-a-cake routines with palms directed to their own bodies, to scraping food from a spoon with their teeth rather than letting their lips mould into the spoon and so on. All these have been reported in autism but there is no systematic evidence on their specificity to, or universality within, the condition.

Movements themselves may be performed in odd ways, either with too much or too little muscle tension. Again, it is not clear what leads to these inconsistencies and how far they are attributable to autism or related conditions. They differ from forms of cerebral palsy in that the child does not have generally weak or rigid muscle tone but appears to be limp on some occasions and rigid on others. Teachers will often attribute this to different levels of motivation for different tasks, but this does not seem to us to be the complete answer. There does appear to be at least some connection with intentionality so that difficulties in intending actions also mean that the effort and energy necessary to carry them out are not marshalled at the planning stage. Actions that are triggered unconsciously will automatically receive the energy output and the effort needed for their execution. The limp behaviour associated with prompted work tasks, on the other hand, may have a motivational component as well as resulting from the very dependent learning style pupils are being encouraged to adopt.

Difficulties in intending will lead to hesitancy and dependence on physical prompting, or at least visual cueing, to get actions started. Dyspraxic conditions mean that automatic unplanned actions can be performed effectively but that actions that require voluntary effort are impossible. This leads to situations where children can pick up a cup and drink from it as long as they are responding automatically to the sight of the cup and the fact that they are thirsty. But as soon as they are directed to pick up the cup (without any physical prompt to do so) or they want to do so in a deliberate way, they cannot execute the action. Teachers and carers who are not familiar with dyspraxic conditions, not surprisingly, see such behavioural inconsistency as an example of 'difficult' and 'negative' behaviour.

Difficulties in crossing thresholds may relate to similar problems but may also arise from perceptual difficulties. We have already seen how even able individuals like Donna Williams can have difficulty in taking in the information about a room visually, without some support from the proximal senses.[33] Certainly, many children with autism appear to be made anxious by large unstructured spaces and simply placing a mat or piece of tape across the division between two rooms may help the pupil to enter the new space. In the same way, a large hall space can be made manageable by dividing it with barriers or giving the pupil a designated (and physically marked, perhaps with a hoop or by a mat) space to occupy. Failure to break up the space in this way will often lead to the hugging of the perimeters of the hall or playground or to anxious pacing up and down.

Many children with autism will benefit from motor education programmes, especially those that encourage body awareness and awareness of others. There are commercially available body awareness programmes and movement programmes that encourage not only self and other awareness but also the development of emotional and creative expression. These can be particularly valuable to the non-verbal child with autism where other avenues for expression are not available.

ATTENTION

A feature of autistic thinking is the way in which individuals attend to certain stimuli with a kind of tunnel attention. Only certain stimuli are seen as going together and those outside this attention tunnel are ignored. Thus, the spoken label of an item emanating from an adult some distance away may not be connected with the item, which would need to be held near the adult's lips for the connection to be made.

The problem also relates to the perceived meaning of a task and how this is attributed. Children may perform very well in some tests of analytical perception in that they may be able to disembed triangles hidden within a picture of a pram very effectively. The problem is that they may not have 'seen' the pram in the first place. Their thinking style in this respect therefore makes them good at certain kinds of activity but less effective at others. Unfortunately, the kinds of task at which they excel are often not those that are most highly prized by society in general while those at which they are least effective are precisely the ones that are most useful in academic and more general learning. It also makes them vulnerable in key life skills areas when normally salient features of the environment may be ignored while those which might seem trivial are concentrated upon. For example, the child might ignore a speeding vehicle moving into the centre of visual range while remaining fascinated by a flickering neon sign at the periphery.

At a conceptual level children with autism sometimes develop an intense interest in one precise aspect of a subject area while remaining indifferent to related issues which would seem to hold a similar attraction. These tend to be described as obsessional interests though they are really only a natural product of a style of thinking that is highly attention-specific. Often, children with autism are described as being 'poor in concentration' or as having an 'attentional deficit'; in reality, of course, they often have an extremely high level of concentration and they attend very closely. The problem is that they do not always concentrate on what teachers want them to concentrate upon and neither do they necessarily attend to the topic that the teacher wishes them to attend to. The focus of their attention remains idiosyncratic; it is not necessarily amenable to social direction.

A feature of non-autistic thinking is that attention can be shared between objects and similarly that attention comes under the individual's control and can then be directed according to the demands of the social situation. Within autistic thinking a contrary position exists: attention cannot be shared readily between objects and attention is unconstrained by social context. Recent research into the neuropsychology of autism by Eric Courchesne has related attentional problems to abnormal brain structure and he has argued that a simple delay in switching attention would lead to many of the developmental difficulties associated with autism.[3]

It is important to recognise both the strengths and the difficulties that are presented by this kind of attentional pattern. Its strengths relate to the advantages that accrue from high levels of concentration: e.g. ability to learn considerable amounts of material. The difficulties that arise are that high levels are not necessarily flexible and they cannot always be harnessed and used as we might wish. In the long term it may be that we accept the strength in autism and look to trying to place the students in work situations where their ability to concentrate on one area and to become extremely knowledgeable in it is a usable currency.

FAILURE TO GENERALISE LEARNING

Pupils will need to be taught specifically to transfer their knowledge and skills to new situations; this may be done through practice and 'overlearning' and then retraining in a variety of new situations. Even so, generalisation is likely to be problematic and therefore important life skills are best taught in a functional context (i.e. where skill is used meaningfully). More fundamentally, gain in this respect will occur if pupils are taught to become aware of their own learning strategies through self-reflection.

When teaching for generalisation in autism, teachers need to remain aware of particular difficulties. Thus, failure to appreciate the intentions of others, difficulties in understanding social meaning and a lack of relatedness to the world (whereby categorisation is by perceptual features rather than social and personal meaning) mean that conceptual development will be idiosyncratic. Confusions can be exacerbated if the teacher is unaware of these conceptual differences and offers linguistic labels for what are presumed to be conventional categorisations.

As an example, assume the teacher wishes to teach the concept and the verbal label 'cup' to a child with autism and severe learning difficulties. Following a behavioural approach, the teacher might decide to tackle the task in the following steps:

- A prototypical cup is shown to the child and the teacher says 'Look! Here is a cup. Cup'. The child is allowed to inspect the cup while the teacher repeats the word 'Cup'. This is repeated a number of times.
- The cup is then presented to the child alongside a perceptually very different object, for example, a brick. The teacher says to the child 'Show me the cup! Cup' and prompts the child to respond correctly, if he or she does not do so spontaneously, or shows the wrong object. This step is repeated until the child is performing spontaneously and correctly to some set criterion (say, nine times out of ten). The relative positions of cup and brick are randomly changed to guard against a simple position strategy.
- The brick is then replaced with an object more related to the cup (e.g. plate or spoon) and the previous step is repeated.
- There is another stage of repetition with the contrasting object being related to the cup both by common association and perceptually (perhaps a bowl in a similar material and colour).
- A third object is added so that the cup must now be selected from a display of three.

- A process of generalisation is begun whereby the cup that has been used in the training is replaced with a similar, but not identical cup.
- Other cups are used, each progressively different from the one before until the child is able to select a cup on command, using a wide range of different cups.
- The training sessions are now generalised so the child can perform successfully at different times of the day, with different people, in different situations and so on.

After this exhaustive training programme, the teacher might think that the child should now have a firm concept of a cup and know the word for it. Yet, for the pupil with autism, this might not be the case (or indeed the teacher may never be able to get the pupil to progress beyond the second step, in spite of what appears to be adequate intellectual capability). This might be put down to a lack of motivation or negativism or simply to some unexplained characteristic of autistic functioning. But keen readers of this book may already have spotted the opportunities for confusion, for pupils with autism, in this scenario.

Firstly, the child may never reach criterion in discriminating cup from brick (note that he/she in fact does not need to understand the word in order to do this task, since the correct item is constant) even though it is clear from the way the child gets a drink that he or she is capable of doing so. One possible reason is, as noted earlier, the use of the word 'show'. Not understanding what is required, the child may simply respond to the overall situation and pick up and fiddle with objects at random.

Another possibility is that the child does not understand the feedback on the correct response. Pupils with autism are liable to miss or misinterpret teacher praise or other signs of approval or pleasure. If a tangible reward is offered it may not *be* a reward for that child (tastes are often very idio-syncratic). If it is not functionally related to the cup (as a drink, served in the cup, would be) the child may not recognise the contingent relationship between selection of the cup and the proffering of a reward. Finally, a chance response rate and its associated reward pattern may be perfectly acceptable to the child. Without expectations of getting things 'right' and being rewarded for it, responding by chance at the second stage in the scenario would mean the child was 'correct' 50% of the time and the child may see no reason to alter his or her behaviour on this basis. After all people go on doing the football pools with a far lower payoff rate than 50%.

Yet another possibility is that the child fails at the third stage, i.e. when the brick is changed. Again, it is unlikely to be a failure in discrimination, but a change in the context in which the discrimination of the cup is to be made, that causes the difficulty. It may take even longer to train this new step than it did to train the original discrimination because the change might have led to stress, which disrupts the learning. Frustratingly, each time there is a change, however slight, this pattern could be repeated and instead of each step becoming easier, it might be harder because of the additional stress of further change.

For children with autism, however, the most likely stumbling block will come at the sixth step. For less able children especially, the concept of 'cup' and the associated label will have no general categorical or functional meaning whereby they can relate the object to their own purposes as 'something to drink from'. Instead, they will respond to it as a unique object. So, unless the new cup is so similar that it could be perceptually mistaken for the old, this step will involve them in starting again with new objects and having to cope with the added confusion of having the new object labelled with the same word as before.

Whatever the teacher does in terms of making the situation easier, generalisation of learning is always going to be a problem unless the fundamental difficulties in learning that we addressed earlier have been overcome. What may help, however, is to avoid this kind of discrimination learning procedure, which only adds to problems by encouraging isolated learning steps. In a more cognitive approach the child would not learn about a particular object and then be required to 'unlearn' its particularity while learning a more general concept. Instead, the broader concept would be introduced from the beginning, teaching the child to pay attention to meaning from the start. Thus, instead of being introduced to one cup, the child would be given a vast range to play with and then encouraged to sort them (from a pile of other objects) into a box labelled with a picture of an assortment of cups. The word 'cup' would be introduced only when the child demonstrates by sorting spontaneously and successfully that the concept is established.

ENCOURAGING PUPILS TO THINK

PROBLEM SOLVING

Problem solving is not limited to, for example, 'mathematical sums'. It is a term which encompasses the whole range of problems that the learner is faced with in life. People try to solve problems that are practical, social, emotional, intellectual and so on, all of the time. So, as we use the term below, it is important that teachers accept the term in its widest sense. For the pupil with autism, problems of how to queue up for a meal in a self-service cafeteria may be as significant and as complex as those of a mathematical nature, and for some individuals, of course, the former problems will be infinitely more difficult to resolve than the latter.

A FACILITATORY APPROACH

Bearing in mind all that we have said about autistic thinking so far, it is clear that the teacher is going to have to create a context for learning that is special, regardless of physical location. The specialness will need to revolve around ways of getting children into a position where they can begin to think of themselves as problem solvers and where they begin to develop ways of acting with some independence in problem-solving situations.

Teachers of all children need to establish a sense of trust between their pupils and themselves which extends to a mutual understanding and acceptance of pupils' cognitive and social abilities, and learning potential. It is difficult to imagine how one could trust another person without any idea of what they are thinking about and what their intentions might be. And clearly this is the position of the child with autism. From the teachers' perspective then, children with autism are both more vulnerable to feelings of anxiety about the world of schooling and more difficult to convince that they themselves are understood and accepted. The way forward is to work within the autistic style of thinking, which requires a kind of dependable regularity of response. What teachers need to do therefore is to make themselves as dependable and predictable as possible. Of course, they may build in unpredictability as a teaching device but this will be in a controlled way and will be intentional rather than unintentional.

In a mainstream class, for example, a teacher may always sit at his or her desk to hear children read during a set period of the day. This can be comforting to the child with autism who knows where to go for support, but the teacher may want to change the routine to fit some other purpose (monitor groups of children reading, perhaps). If this is done without warning, the child with autism may become confused and agitated because he or she no longer trusts the teacher to be there when needed. The teacher needs to recognise this need in the pupil explicitly, and explain in detail how the pupil can make contact whenever there is a need, in spite of the change of routine. The teacher needs to realise that the child with autism is not able to trust someone as an individual or as a particular role, nor to trust his or her own capacity to operate in changed circumstances, but needs to be able to trust a pattern of behaviour, which must, therefore, be made predictable. So, trust is important to gain and though it may have to be gained in an artificial kind of way it is nonetheless real for all that.

CHALLENGE WITHOUT PENALTY

The classroom learning (problem-solving) environment should be as non-threatening as possible. Pupils with autism need to learn how to experiment and there should be no sense in which they are penalised for so doing. If problem-solving activities are to help the thinking of the pupil with autism, then they have to be challenging. This means that initial failures may occur particularly if learners try to use a set approach. We know that learners with autism, in particular, tend to use set approaches that have been correct in the past and we know that they find initial failure debilitating, in part at least because they often do not have recourse to alternative strategies. Therefore the teacher needs to structure tasks in such a way that the pupil is not penalised for what the teacher 'intends', nor for what is the result of a key feature of their particular style of thinking and learning. Failure must be accompanied with clear cues for an alternative and more appropriate response, at least initially.

For example, a young boy with autism and severe learning difficulties was taught to buy a favourite chocolate bar from a local shop, by selecting what he wanted from the display, queuing up, and paying with a 20p piece given to him in a purse containing other coins. Clearly, there had been many stages in learning to solve this particular problem, but the boy could now perform it successfully. Further learning, therefore, would challenge this solution, but was necessary if the learning was to have more flexibility and to be useful in other situations. The teacher decided to introduce the first challenge by not giving the child a 20p piece, but giving him instead an equivalent selection of coins (one 10p and two 5p pieces) in the purse. Just to give him these, however, might have resulted in panic in the boy, making him unable to purchase his chocolate bar and thus being penalised for his 'failure'. On the other hand, giving him the right coins, instead of letting him get them from the purse, might have helped him accept their equivalence, but in an unthinking way that would not involve real learning. It would have been a step away from independence in selecting his own coins and he would not have had the necessary emotional reaction, to the failure to find the 20p piece, that would have enabled purposeful searching for an alternative.

The solution was to give him extensive training in the classroom in finding, first the 20p piece and then the remaining coins in the purse equivalent to the 20p (one 10p and two 5ps). Each time, he would be shown the chocolate bar wrapper and asked for 20p to pay for it. Back in the real situation of the shop, then, he did react with momentary panic when there was no 20p piece in his purse, but the chocolate wrapper was there to remind him of the significance of the remaining coins in the purse and with a look of triumph (or so it seemed to the teacher, looking on) he handed over the coins and received his chocolate bar.

THE IMPORTANCE OF FEEDBACK

The feedback given to pupils needs to be as non-threatening as possible (remembering the range of things that may be threatening in autism) and needs to relate to the pupils' own role in the task so that they can focus upon it. It is a matter of teacher judgement as to the point within any task at which there is a need for feedback and when there needs to be time allowed for further experimentation. Teachers may need to intervene when it is clear that a child's responses to the problem are random and unlikely to produce a correct response. But the timing and nature of that intervention is critical. Children with autism will sometimes produce a response long after one would normally expect it. Children need to be shown how their unsuccessful response related to the problem and they need to have the successful problem-solving procedure modelled for them so that they can relate it to their own performance and their own potentialities.

This point can be illustrated by a girl with autism who had a rather flamboyant attitude to cooking, especially where it involved the addition of seasonings. She seemed unwilling or unable to judge small quantities of these (such as half a teaspoon) and would merrily continue pouring until stopped. The teacher was concerned that she would never reach any degree of independence if someone always needed to intervene in this way, so she had been allowed to empty a container of pepper into her dinner one day in the hope that the resulting inedibility would make her more responsive to direction in the future. This was a risky strategy in that many pupils with autism might not even notice that the food was supposed to be inedible. However, in this case that part of the strategy worked in that she refused to eat the dinner but no amount of verbal explanations of the role of the pepper in this seemed to impinge and there was no effect on later performance. The feedback on the 'mistake' was too remote to be effective.

Next time, her meal was divided in two and she was once more allowed to empty the pepper container into one half. Immediately after doing so she was encouraged to taste the dinner and to taste a tiny bit of the pepper to make the connection. She was then shown how to pour the right amount of pepper into a spoon (and given several trials at this) before being allowed to pour the right amount into the second portion of her meal and taste that. The learning needed reinforcement and generalisation to other seasonings and different meals, but this time she learnt quickly and her behaviour became more purposeful and controlled. Feedback was made relevant in this case and the correct alternative made available. Ignoring incorrect responses (which is effectively what was happening in the first strategy) is unlikely to be effective in this respect. It is not enough for them to know that they are wrong; they need to know why and how to put it right.

LEARNING TO BE MOTIVATED

As pupils become more aware of their repertoire of problem-solving responses, then they need to be given more responsibility for their own learning. They should be encouraged to take control of aspects within the problem-solving situation for themselves rather than seeing adults as the sole repository of information and solutions. For example, at a low level they might physically take charge of the materials needed to make a Christmas card when working with an adult; at a higher level they might specifically be given the task of choosing when to go to the dictionary to look up the spelling of a word (this becomes part of the defined roles within an activity rather than a presupposed function of being the learner). They need to learn to appreciate the usefulness or otherwise of strategies they adopt and they need to have some way of revising or correcting unsuccessful attempts without necessarily having recourse to adults' judgements and advice.

Getting children (and not just those with autism) to tidy their rooms can become a continual process of nagging, which is far from the independence teachers and carers would like to see in this area. Apart from the normal motivational problems attendant on this task, children with autism face the added difficulty of not understanding what 'tidy' means and thus having no clear conception of what they are supposed to be doing. This can be solved by providing a picture of the room when it is in a tidy condition (or several pictures, if this is necessary) so the child has a clear goal to work towards and an independent way of checking when the goal has been reached.

Similarly, children with autism need to learn that the reward for completing a task does not always reside with the teacher. It is an important part of learning to be motivated that they learn to get satisfaction from completing the task for themselves. Teachers may need to develop ways of enabling pupils to learn to give themselves rewards for task completion (which might be time for a favoured activity) as an artificial way of beginning to understand about being motivated by success; which is something, again, that non-autistic people tend to operate on but not recognise.

A STRUCTURE FOR MAKING DECISIONS

Because of the nature of autistic thinking individuals with autism tend to become readily dependent on the teacher or any alternative structure that is set up. Teachers cannot ignore this dependency and expect their pupils suddenly to become independent learners. Learners with autism need structure which they can rely on and within which they can learn to make decisions. What may appear as laziness, or a lack of knowledge or motivation, could be a difficulty in recognising and using their own judgement. The prop to aid independent thinking may be a set of pictures or a diagram or a list but whatever it is, the child needs to learn to use the prop on trial runs where the 'risks' are low. In this way he or she might be enabled to develop more control, and to appreciate that he or she can make decisions. The step-up in learning comes when the children become aware that they are using a prop and when they begin to choose to use it on some occasions and not on others; for example, when they are aware that they can write a shopping list and when they choose to do so for shopping trips where the list is long but not where there is only one item to buy.

EMPHASISING THE POSITIVE

Children with autism are no different from others in responding more productively when corrections emphasise what to do rather than what not to do. All education should emphasise the positive, but it is especially important where an emphasis on stopping or suppressing behaviour leaves the child without any idea of what to put in its place. The child with autism stands to benefit more significantly than others from a positive approach when the mutuality of positive learning experiences is stressed. Teachers, then, need to model enjoyment in the doing of tasks. They need to create a genuinely enjoyable mutual experience in which it is made clear to the child that the learning is mutual, that it is enjoyable and that he or she is part of that enjoyable scenario.

THE TEACHER AS ONGOING MODEL

Following on from the above we suggest that when working with individuals with autism, teaching by modelling is likely to be an effective approach. Sharing an activity with the pupil (for example, the teacher making her own clay pot while the child is making one) enables that mutuality of experiences, as well as providing a context in which the child can make judgements of the teacher's work, or even make helpful suggestions, rather than just being the recipient of them.

REFLECTING ON ENJOYMENT

Because of the importance of emotion in learning and the difficulties of this in autism, it is clear that reflection on enjoyment needs to be a specific curriculum aim rather than simply a hoped for product of schooling. Many pupils with autism need to be taught how to enjoy themselves. An academic agenda may come to dominate learning situations to such an extent that learning about enjoyment, if not entirely precluded, is certainly not encouraged. Teachers may move children on to the next stage in learning as soon as a successful threshold has been reached, without necessarily giving them a chance to enjoy the thing that has just been learnt. The current emphasis on accountability encourages this kind of relentless progression through targets. Children with autism cannot afford to waste precious learning time, but teachers must recognise the value of learning about enjoyment itself as an aim.

Certainly, enjoyment appears in the curriculum when adolescents do leisure activities and so on, but we suggest that it actually needs to be an overt part of the formal curriculum at a much younger age. In our view then, enjoyment is a legitimate educational aim and hurrying on from it for 'educational' purposes may be to miss the point. Pupils need to reflect on enjoyment, and to learn to share that with others. Adults can encourage sharing by ensuring eye contact at the appropriate time, mirroring the child's enjoyment by the adult's expression and, for those with some understanding of speech, pointing out to the pupil that he or she is happy. Also, a photograph of the happy experience will provide a cue for later reflection. Again, this notion is an important part of our wider concern that we as teachers should draw pupils' attention to their own experiences rather than always to features within the task itself.

TEACHING PROBLEM-SOLVING STRATEGIES

COPING WITH INCREASING PROBLEM-SOLVING DEMANDS

Teachers need to remain aware that different dimensions contribute to task difficulty and that children with autism have particular difficulty in coping with changes in more than one dimension at a time. Teachers also need to recognise that what counts as a difficulty will be idiosyncratic but nonetheless real. Problems usually arise because teachers are unaware of the complexities, in terms of different dimensions, in the tasks they present. Earlier chapters saw how this can arise in the teaching of communication and a similar example can be given for teaching mathematics.

Children usually come to number first through experience of ordinal numbers (numbers in sequence) through counting experiences of climbing stairs and so on. When teachers start to teach number groups (cardinal numbers) they will usually draw on the child's ordinal knowledge to get them to make cardinal judgements in that they will ask the question 'How many?' of a group of items and get the child to count them one by one to reach the answer. All children may experience difficulty with this as the last number they count suddenly has to switch roles from the last in a sequence to the collective 'name' for all the items in the group. Children with autism, however, have additional handicaps in that they will not be able to 'read' the teacher's intentions, they will not pick up the social signals that provide clues to the change in the nature of the task, and their learning is more rigidly attached to its original circumstances. It is not surprising, therefore, if a painstaking count of one to five still leads to an 'eight' (or other inappropriate response) to the question 'How many?' The problem needs to be tackled by giving separate training in making cardinal judgements, using very small numbers to begin with, that can be perceived at a glance. We have found that one useful way of controlling levels of difficulty is to use computer learning environments with appropriate software.[16, 26]

SOCIAL AND AFFECTIVE DEMANDS

Following on from the above it is also clear that where the social dimension is facilitatory in normally developing pupils, this may well not be the case with children with autism. Indeed, here social interaction may militate against further understanding. We question then if it is sensible to try to teach interactive skills at the same time as something else. Whatever the case, when we teach pupils with autism we need to allow for the social and affective resources that are also being demanded. As we have suggested elsewhere, computer-assisted learning or the structuring of tasks to such a degree that they can be tackled independently, may be useful for learning new or difficult material. It is also easier for the child with autism to learn from a familiar adult who will have learnt to reduce the social demands made on the child, than to learn from 'co-operation' with peers.

DEVELOPING SELECTIVE ATTENTION

We saw earlier that children with autism do not develop joint attention in the 'automatic' way that is typical of children without autism. This early impairment leads to a general difficulty with shared attention and to having their attention directed by others. They may simply be unaware of the significance of conventional gestures such as holding objects up for inspection, pointing to them or even the use of language to direct attention. Activities designed for pupils with autism, then, will need to incorporate the directing of attention by varying degrees of forceful encouragement.

This may involve building visual mechanisms that direct attention into activities, such as highlighting the key elements in a text in a way that illustrates its structure (highlighting the main character in a particular colour, for example, and then using that colour to pick out each reference to that character whether it be by name, pronoun or other noun phrase). At a less advanced level, it would be using pictorial timetables of the day where each activity could be turned over or covered up as completed, drawing the child's attention to the next activity in the sequence.

But again the step-up in learning is when the pupils begin to direct their own attention. In the first of the examples given, the pupils will need to learn to highlight the roles in the text for themselves and eventually to be able to attend to such features of the text without highlighting at all. Equally, in the second example, the pupils could progress from turning over a card for themselves, to crossing through a picture, to placing a tick beside the completed task picture and finally to mentally noting the completed task and directing attention to the next one. Pupils with autism need experience in directing their own attention where they are shown what they are doing and how they are doing it, so that they can begin to take control of their own ways of attending in future related problem-solving situations.

ATTENDING TO MEANING

It is clear that in autism children do not readily search for meaning (or at least not conventional meaning) in the way that is typical of non-autistic learners. Therefore teachers of those with autism need to teach 'attention to meaning' explicitly, otherwise there is a danger of simply teaching a range of procedural habits. Selective attention should therefore involve attending to the purpose of the event. For example, in reflecting on a series of photographs depicting an activity just undertaken (making a sandwich) the pupil's attention could be focused away from labelling items in the photograph, or repeating learnt phrases, to giving a one word description of the 'gist' of the activity being undertaken.

Selective attention to meaning also implies recognising irrelevancy at the planning stage of a task and the pupils will need specific practice in this. Instead of the teacher setting out the materials needed for a particular task (such as cleaning a table) a pupil can be offered initially the essential equipment (a rag, some container for water and a cleaning agent) plus an obviously irrelevant item (such as a hairbrush or a long-handled broom). The pupil is then taught to select consciously at this stage rather than by default in simply not using the unwanted item. Difficulty can be increased by adding items and extending this to other tasks, including more academic ones where the irrelevancy is not so visually apparent. Planning a task, including planning the equipment needed to carry it out, should be as much part of the classroom routine as reflection on tasks completed.

DEFINING THE PROBLEM

Learners should not be presented with problems that they cannot solve because they do not have the required skill or knowledge or because it is beyond the range of their abilities in any respect. This is a matter of very fine judgement on the part of the teacher; for a problem to be at all useful as a way of learning it needs to be not immediately solvable (it has to be 'problematic' by definition) but it also has to be resolvable by the individual at the time it is presented.

Herein is the particularity of the difficulty of the autistic thinker. What might be resolvable at one time might not be at another simply because the information needed is not available at that time (because it has not been cued by the situation) and anything more than the finest of gradations of difficulty may render a problem irresolvable for a particular individual. Teachers should be aware that it is not enough that the pupil has been taught a particular necessary skill, the pupil must also have a way of gaining access to that skill. In other words, the pupil must know that he or she knows.

There is an additional difficulty for those individuals with autism who do develop an awareness of themselves as problem solvers in that the awareness that develops may include a perception of themselves as inadequate in this respect. Thus, if they are not shown clearly what they know and how to go about retrieving that information and applying it to problems, they may only develop a form of 'learned helplessness' where they immediately give up when faced with any difficulty and wait for the teacher to take over. Teachers of those with autism therefore need to take care in how they present problem-solving activities. Many of those with autism who have expectations tend to have expectations of failure, but if the problem is clearly defined, they are less likely to attribute failure of a particular strategy to their own perceived inadequacies and be more willing to try another one.

DEVELOPING A RANGE OF STRATEGIES FOR MEMORISING AND RETRIEVING INFORMATION

The teacher of those with autism needs to ensure that pupils have a range of strategies for memorising and retrieving information (which might include for example: classification, rehearsal, visualisation techniques, semantic elaboration, and the development of 'scripts' or 'schema'). It is only when a range is available that future self-selection from that range (which is the step-up in learning that we would seek if we truly wanted to improve thinking) can occur.

Each of these strategies will need specific teaching, within the child's capacity to learn. It should be remembered that 'rehearsal', for example, need not be limited to those with language since an 'object of reference' will help the non-verbal child with additional learning difficulties to keep in mind the reason he or she is leaving the classroom (going to the toilet, going swimming, and so on) and will lead to less anxiety as well as providing training in remembering. Of course, this only provides short bursts of memory, continually cued by the object, but it is a start. Overt gestures that mirror an appropriate action associated with the activity (like a very iconic sign) would serve the same function for a slightly more able child (or the same child at a later time) and have the advantage of being more abstract and therefore involving more opportunities for cognitive growth.

DEVELOPING BOTH LINGUISTIC AND NON-LINGUISTIC WAYS OF TEACHING

Pupils with autism often have associated language problems, and this affects the way they can use language to help them classify and use information. Traditionally, education has focused on the use of verbal strategies in thinking but visual strategies may have equal value and certainly pupils with autism may find them particularly helpful. For example, pupils can be helped to recall sequences of events, or to plan future activities, through the use of pictures depicting stages in those events. This is particularly valuable in helping those with language difficulties become aware of the steps they have taken to solve a problem and to reflect on their own strategies.

There is a need for this kind of visual mediation when planning an activity and when debriefing the pupil afterwards. It is also important to note that, in autism, skills such as the use of language may seem to be available to pupils but, under circumstances which are stressful to them, the general level of skill competence may be reduced. Thus a pupil who 'has' the ability to read may not be able to access it when in a stressful situation. For example, a pupil given a written shopping list because he 'can read', may find it impossible to do so in the (for him) stressful context of the shop. What he needs then is a visual 'list', a set of pictures of items that he needs so that he can function effectively even in the stressful situation. In short, in autism the availability of skills and knowledge to an individual is not dependable and will vary according to context and time and, again, the social dimension is often the significant one.

AWARENESS OF OWN THINKING

DEVELOPING A VARIETY OF APPROACHES

One of the key features of autism in general is a liking for sameness, at least where the overall situation is familiar. Thus, children may welcome total change (going on holiday) but be severely disturbed by the removal of a picture from the classroom wall. Similarly, a key feature of autistic thinking is a tendency to adopt the same strategy even when the problem has changed in such a way as to demand a different one. In order to improve the effectiveness of autistic thinking then, one needs to find ways of discouraging pupils from accepting one particular rule or searching for particular knowledge and to encourage them to approach a problem with the notion that a range of rules could apply.

It may be possible to make the task one in which two ways have to be found to complete it successfully. A simple version of this is making up the correct money for a purchase with different combinations of coins to establish the notion of equivalence (2 plus 2 equals 4, but so does 3 plus 1, or

5 minus 1 and so on). This also needs to be extended to much larger strategies for problem solving in, for example, shopping for a meal. One approach is to decide on the meal, look up the ingredients needed, check what is already in store and devise a shopping list based on the order that appears in the list of ingredients. The sorting out of where to get what is then done on the shopping trip on a one-by-one basis by going down the list. This is a reasonable strategy for supermarket shopping and has the advantage of keeping the items categorised by their role in the meal, providing a memory structure for later recall of what was bought.

However, it is a disastrous method for use with specialist shops some distance apart and each with a queue. Imagine queuing for the vegetables in the greengrocers at one end of the parade, going off to the butchers, back again for fruit, and so on. Here, the organisation of the list needs to take account of the way goods are categorised for selling, rather than their role in the meal, and it is that categorisation that will provide the later cue for reflection. The step-up in thinking will come when the pupil has both organisational strategies available and can choose the most appropriate for the circumstances for him or herself.

Teachers need to encourage pupils to acquire a repertoire of responses, to be aware of this repertoire and to understand the need for flexibility. In real life situations it is often a matter of weighing the advantages and disadvantages of different approaches, rather than looking for a single correct answer or even one correct approach. Getting pupils to develop a variety of approaches is difficult because it 'goes against the grain' of autistic thinking and can cause stress. It needs to be considered, therefore, at the planning or reflection stage of a teaching and learning episode rather than during the activity itself. For example, thinking of another sequence for purchasing items makes no sense when you have already purchased them in a particular order. But it may be useful to think about ways of sequencing the shopping before leaving for the shop or, at the reflection stage, to think of other ways of finding items if the shop arrangement has been changed.

DEVELOPING LEARNING STYLES THAT INCORPORATE MORE ADVANCED STRATEGIES

Because learning for the child with autism often seems so difficult it may seem that we should accept a successful performance on a task as the best that the child can achieve in terms of their difficulties. And we have already said how important it is to resist the temptation always to be pushing ahead to the next phase of learning. But there is a complementary need in autism to continually look for ways of incorporating more advanced strategies into the child's repertoire. This need is particularly pressing in autism where learning style does not always develop without intervention from outside.

So children with autism may be enabled to progress from scanning to focusing by engaging in problem-solving tasks that give them experience in recognising and disregarding information which is irrelevant to the problem. The kinds of strategies used in selecting for meaning are also applicable here.

The purpose here is to look for overall meaning and to make guesses or judgements about the situation based on this notion of meaning. In other words they should pay less attention to the purely perceptual features of a situation but learn to take an attitude to it that searches for relevance in what they are seeing. In this way they may learn to focus on relevant features in order to try out hypotheses, rather than relying on a haphazard scanning of the situation. At a simple level this can be developed through categorisations of objects or events based on functional or more abstract qualities, rather than on appearance. Incorporating a personal affective element will also be helpful. Thus, children can sort objects into things to wear versus things to eat but then further categorise each of these groups into 'things I like to eat/wear' versus 'things I don't like to eat/wear'.

What we are suggesting here, then, is that teachers need to continually analyse tasks to see how they might be adapted to further develop advanced strategies in their pupils, and importantly the analysis needs to be made in the light of what we know about autistic thinking. There is no magic formula that can be applied to the teaching of pupils with autism and, in our view, no predetermined set of activities that will enhance their thinking performance. It is a matter of stepping back from activities that are to be presented and analysing how they relate to autistic thinking and how they can be utilised to facilitate the development of that thinking.

USING A RANGE OF STRATEGIES FOR MEMORISING AND RETRIEVING INFORMATION

All children have to come to recognise that some things need to be memorised and that they need to identify an appropriate strategy that will help them with that memorisation. Many children with autism will not do this spontaneously and will need direct teaching in order to do so. And again, in order to improve their thinking ability they need to develop their own control over this process. Therefore they need to have practice in selecting and using strategies for memorising and retrieving information that will be appropriate to different situations and given ways of reflecting on that practice. For example, rehearsal would be an appropriate strategy for remembering a short message, whereas remembering a story would require constructing a schema of the main characters and events. As we saw in the section on narrative development, this will need specific training. Situations, therefore, need to be arranged wherein this distinction is valid and then that distinction needs to be deliberately explicated either verbally or visually.

REFLECTING ON EXPERIENCE

This underpins the whole notion of a cognitive curriculum and while it is dealt with here separately it is also incorporated in many of the other sections. Tasks given to pupils with autism (and the way in which they are presented) need to give them opportunities to increase their awareness of their own ways of handling problem situations. Learners with autism firstly need to establish that they do or do not know; the step up for them comes when they can be helped to bridge the gap between this knowledge that they do not know, and their knowledge of why they do not know.

Completion of a task should not be seen as the end of learning; the learner with autism has a particular need for time, and facilitation where appropriate, in order to reflect on the method he/she has used in solving the problem and to consider alternatives. Teachers need to build into session plans periods of reflection which involve the mnemonics that could be useful, or have been useful, at particular points in the problem-solving episode. They also need to try to make the reflection that does occur, include reflection on the emotional aspects of the task. What is needed is for pupils to reflect (rather than merely review or recall) and to this end they need to come to make evaluative judgements about what they have been doing. In our own work we have been using instant photographs to capture pupils' own actions and facial expressions as a first step in the process.

The cake going into the oven might be the trigger for the teacher to sit with the pupils and go over the cake-making exercise (using pictures where appropriate) rather than the trigger for washing up and getting ready to eat it. At this stage, the memories are fresher and the children can be helped to pay attention to and identify the significance of the smells that come from the oven as the cake is cooking. They can readily anticipate the next stage in the process (the eating of the cake) because there are lots of cues and they will find the purpose of the cake-making personally relevant (providing they like cake). There will also be signs around (flour spilt on the floor, mixture on their lips from the licking of the bowl, and so on) to provide cues for their episodic memory of the event and these can be built on by the teacher to make sure the memories are accessible on future occasions of cake-making. None of this will have the same import if the 'reflection' occurs after the cake has been eaten, in another room far removed from the sights and smells of the original experience and the eager anticipation of eating the cake that will give emotional engagement to the task.

Similarly, we have found that a very good way to get pupils to reflect, or at least recall, is by getting them to help peers or other 'naïve' teachers with a task that they have recently completed themselves. Re-enacting situations in this way enables pupils to at least get into the position of reflecting on how to do something.

Getting children to reflect on a personal event can be done through the kind of structuring of the event that we saw was necessary in the section on narratives. For example, in the home context, after returning from a shopping trip, the mother might sit with the child as they look at what they have bought (to act as a trigger for the memories) and ask about the trip. The child would be asked such questions as 'Do you remember the shop where we bought this? Did you like trying it on? Do you remember the other one you tried? Did it fit? Did you like the colour? Why did you prefer this one? Were you happy in that shop?' and so on. As the child becomes used to answering such factual questions, albeit with emotional and evaluative undertones, then the questions can be extended to provide more of a structure of the event. The questions will focus on what happened, when, who was there, what people felt or experienced, what happened as a result, and how people felt then. The shopping trip to buy a new coat, then, might be analysed thus:

- Who went shopping?
- Why did we go shopping? (What did we want to buy?)
- Which shop did we go in?
- How did you feel in the shop? (Was it crowded, noisy, bright, etc.?)
- Which coats did we choose to try on?
- Did you like the other ones?
- Why did you choose this one?
- Are you happy to have a new coat?
- Will Daddy think you look smart in your new coat?
- Where will you wear your new coat?

When Daddy returns in the evening, then, the child can be prompted to retell the shopping trip story in this format. In the beginning, the mother may need to go through each of these questions again in order for the child to be able to retell the story, but, as the child becomes more familiar with the format of story telling, it may be enough just to trigger the story by a general prompt such as 'Tell Daddy what we did today, when we went shopping'.

Such a child may then need experience in analysing events that have happened to others (narratives that have been told to him or her) in this way. If he or she can read, then written texts are more useful in establishing the structure of a story because the memory component is removed and key events or key characters in the story can be visually highlighted in some way as a first step in this analysis. The teaching aim is to get the child to listen to or read narratives in such a way that the structure of who, when, what, where, how, why and what next is established automatically as the story unfolds and remains as a kind of précis of the event for later recall. Once the child is giving the structure of an event fairly automatically, when prompted to do so after hearing the narrative, it is time to start introducing prompts when the narrative is being told, to try to get the child to start constructing the model as the story is being told and not to wait until the end when it has to be done from recall. This will produce artificial situations which are probably best tackled first at school where normal communication with the rest of the family is not being disrupted in the process. What is involved is the adult starting to tell a narrative and breaking off at key points to ask a pertinent question of the child such as 'Why did I go to the station?'

Where the child has no spoken language, all this becomes more problematic, but there are still steps that can be taken. Personal events can be recalled through the use of objects, pictures or photographs. To begin with objects can be specific to the situation (e.g. the item bought on a shopping trip, the packet of cereal to prompt recall of breakfast) but a later aim would be to produce 'objects of reference' that would be objects that 'stand for' a whole episode or event. For example, a shopping bag might be used to stand for 'shopping' regardless of what was bought or a particular plate might be used to stand for breakfast, regardless of what was eaten. Pictures or photographs can be used in the same way to highlight key events and characters in the narrative and to provide a way in which the child can demonstrate his or her understanding by sequencing them.

Just as with the use of verbal prompts with the verbal child, it is important that personal narratives are reflected on in a way that involves the individual's experience of the event and does not rely simply on recall of a set of events. It may be harder to elicit emotional or evaluative memories without language, but the photographs, for example, should be of the child undergoing the experience on a particular occasion (that is, they should be instant photographs taken at the time) and not some general representation of the event. In other words, the photographs should help the child relive the experience where attention is drawn (through the captured facial expressions, for example) to how the child was feeling at the time and should not just record the order in which the event unfolded. A set of instant photographs that depict an event that has happened in one setting (home or school), and can be sequenced to 'retell' the event in the other setting, is an excellent (if expensive) way of communicating about daily experiences between home and school. If both settings are aware of how to help the child reflect on these photographs, it will also greatly enhance the child's understanding of the event in question and how to 'talk' about it to others.

ENABLING VERSUS CONTROLLING

There is a real dilemma when teaching pupils with autism in that efforts to help them can easily become measures that control. This is because their learning style leads with a kind of inevitability to dependency and because they often lack the ability to self-direct. What is needed, then, is for the teacher to continually look for ways of enabling rather than controlling the pupil with autism.

For example, if a pupil is distressed then teachers need to help them to cope rather than simply to take over. Again, there is a matter of judgement here. If a pupil became very upset having been sent to get an item that had been moved to a different and unknown location, then to find the new location for him or her would be to reinforce the usual strategy of stopping until the nearest adult takes over. To try to get the child to think of what he or she might do (search/ask/find an alternative, etc.) would be to 'risk' further upset and possible violent reaction. What the teacher in this instance needs to do is to try instead to give more knowledge and confidence in the child's own strategies so that this becomes increasingly less problematic. The decision might be made here that, in the immediate circumstance, the pupil needs to be shown the new location because, on this particular day at this particular time, further upset would be generally counter-productive to any further learning on his or her part or indeed for those in the vicinity. But this decision does not preclude the incident being used for further learning after the event, perhaps by re-enactment or by discussion or by diagrammatic representation.

ENABLING LEARNING THROUGH SOCIAL AND EMOTIONAL ROUTES

EMPLOYING EMOTIONAL CUES TO MEMORY

Chapter 3 made clear the case for suggesting that emotion plays a significant part in the development of usable autobiographical memories and that it is within this area that pupils with autism have a major difficulty. Teachers of those with autism therefore need to find ways in which they can enable pupils to recognise and reflect on their emotional states during problem-solving activities as a way of developing awareness of their own role in those activities and thus helping to establish an autobiographical memory.

What is needed then is an emphasis on the evaluative part of reflections; it is not enough that pupils with autism talk about what they have done, the step-up in their learning will come when they make judgements about their part in the activity. This will be easier if cues have been established during the task. Teachers need to be alert for any emotional reaction to the task as it is ongoing (even where the reaction is negative) and to use it for reflection at the time and a cue for later memories. Thus, signs of frustration at a particular point are not met with a hurrying on to the next bit, but are drawn to the child's attention through talking about it, or showing the child his or her expression in a mirror, as appropriate. The words used, or the mirror, may then be used as cues in recall.

MAKING MEANING ACCESSIBLE

Pupils with autism are unable to engage in the game of 'guessing what teacher thinks' which occurs when teachers have a predetermined answer or topic in mind. Rather, teachers of such pupils need either to make meanings explicit through the use of more directive questions, or they need to accept pupils' contributions and attribute meaning and appropriateness to those contributions. This kind of attribution needs to be sustained. That is, teachers need to accept the change in topic rather than trying to return to their original focus. This can be difficult with set curricula such as the National Curriculum, but teachers can perhaps employ ingenuity in their interpretation and be aware that the curriculum priorities of social and communicative development should be just that—priorities.

Teachers of pupils with autism have to recognise that the social relationship is an unequal one with the teacher as 'expert' and the pupil as 'novice'. The teacher's role, therefore, must be one of creating interactions that require only the minimal interactional skills that his/her partner may be capable of at that point.

CONCLUSION

We have suggested in this chapter that children with autism can be taught to think more effectively, although additional learning difficulties and a lack of language ability may set limits on their learning. The problems are wrapped up in the particular way in which autistic memory processes operate, which, in turn, have their roots in the difficulty of establishing and developing an experiencing self. The possibilities for effective teaching are in the area of developing in individuals the ability to reflect on their own role in problem-solving situations. Ways forward are to be found in an analysis of one's own teaching and a looking for ways of extending reflection at the level which is appropriate for the individual at any given time. In the remaining chapters of this book we look to the implications of this kind of cognitive curriculum in terms of how to manage behaviours in autism and how such a curriculum impinges upon the wider social context of autism.

Managing Behaviours

7

BEHAVIOUR PROBLEMS

Behaviour problems are not a unique defining feature of autism but they are strongly associated with it both in quantity and in severity. They are also strongly linked to mental retardation and so individuals who have both autism and severe learning difficulties are very likely to have behaviour problems at some point in their lives (and most commonly at two points—early childhood and adolescence), and those problems are likely to be more severe than for other groups. The kind of behaviour problem will vary according to circumstances and the child's learning history, but also according to the child's personality and degree of autism. Those who are aloof and withdrawn are most likely to respond to frustration with temper tantrums, non-directed aggression and destructiveness. The more 'passive' group will not understand social situations and will not be assertive, so they will tend to be led into trouble by others. Their social naïveté also means that their crimes are easily detected. The 'active but odd' group seek social contact but seldom get it right so they are often teased and bullied.

The high association with epilepsy in autism also means that some forms of disturbed and even aggressive behaviour, that it is believed may be associated with some forms of epilepsy, will be found in autism. Children with autism will also be prone to all the factors that lead to emotional disturbance in others and there is nothing in autism that protects the individual from pre-menstrual tension, anxiety attacks, phobias, or depressions. In fact, as we have seen, the lack of understanding of themselves or others may make them more prone to suffer from these emotional and behavioural disturbances. They are sometimes not recognised or treated in autism and there is a danger that everything may be attributed to the autism. One should also remember that the lack of friendship groups, and of close emotional and empathetic ties with others, means that children with autism do not have the outlet for sharing their troubles and receiving the comfort and reassurance of loved ones, that keeps the rest of us from more severe emotional disorders and enables us to cope with life's traumas.

There are several questions we need to ask about the behaviour before we can decide whether it needs 'management' at all and we always need to look at the role we, and the context, play in creating and maintaining certain behaviours as well as the role played by the individual and his or her autism. Nevertheless, individuals with autism do have a particular perspective on the world and we can only understand and manage their behaviour if we begin to appreciate that perspective.

MANAGING UNWANTED BEHAVIOUR

The first step in managing unwanted or bizarre behaviour, then, lies in understanding it. Let us consider three alternative hypotheses, any one of which might be applicable in a particular situation.

LIMITED BEHAVIOURAL REPERTOIRE

At the simplest level the behaviour may be bizarre simply because it is a low-level response which is all the child has in his or her repertoire. For example, children may twirl the wheels of a car partly because they do not understand the symbolic significance of 'playing cars', or may sniff people because information from olfactory senses is easier for them to interpret than that from vision or auditory channels. If this is understood then the behaviour may no longer seem so bizarre and the problem might 'go away' or at least be redefined as a need to help the child achieve a higher level of cognitive functioning; in short it becomes a cognitive rather than a social difficulty. Teaching the child to rely less on the proximal senses of smell and touch and more on sight and sound, which are more socially acceptable, is breaking new ground and it is an area where there needs to be more co-operation between psychological and biological research. But we would argue here that it may be cruel just to block a child's main way of making sense of the world and to force him or her to use information from senses that he or she may find distorted and confusing.

ENVIRONMENTAL TRIGGER

If the trigger for the unwanted behaviour is identified as a particular noise or level of noise (or colour, or social situation or whatever) then a reasonable hypothesis might be that this is an aversive stimulus for the child who is signalling that by his or her behaviour. If this were to be the case then the behaviour would be, in effect, a primitive form of communication, which would be a very encouraging sign. In such a situation one would want to give the child an alternative way of communicating distress other than through the unwanted behaviour.

BEHAVIOUR AS A BLOCK

A third hypothesis might be that the child is using the behaviour to block out a particular stimulus. If this were the case it might be worthwhile trying to remove the aversive stimulus either directly or by giving the child a proximal block such as ear plugs, though we recognise that this is not always possible or desirable.

An example of determining causation comes from a case study of Adriana, an eight-year-old girl with autism, who would scream and bite the back of her hand for no apparent reason. The first step in this situation, then, was to conduct a functional analysis, analysing the situation in terms of an ABC analysis.

Thus:

- A = antecedents to the behaviour
- B = the behaviour itself (in objective terms, not depending on descriptions such as 'aggressive' or 'self-injuring')
- C = the consequences of the behaviour.

In this case, B was easy to define in terms of a scream followed by biting of the fleshy part of the right hand. Staff had tried a number of different strategies for coping with the behaviour such as ignoring or trying to pacify and distract her but these had not affected the occurrence of the behaviour. Thus C was not easily identifiable in terms of a consequence that was reinforcing or maintaining the behaviour.

Attention then turned to A, the events leading to or 'triggering' the behaviour. By making careful timed observations in a variety of settings over a number of different occasions, it became clear that the trigger was the word sound [no]. This had been missed by her teachers because she not only responded to 'no' (which might have been understandable given its relationship with prohibition or refusal) but also to the homophone 'know' even when it was overheard in conversations directed to others. The behaviour still needed to be modified but now it could be seen as a more meaningful response to Adriana's interpretation of a particular sound: a sound associated with frustration of her actions.

Having argued for a functional analysis, it is also clear that this is often a very difficult analysis to carry out in the context of autism. Precisely because behaviours do not always follow the pattern of cause and effect that we normally expect, so it is difficult to pin down just what it is about situations that is triggering a particular behaviour. In many ways it is a matter of suspending our disbelief, of trying to stand outside of our intuitive understanding of behavioural responses and imagining what may be happening.

LEARNING NEEDS ARISING FROM RIGIDITY IN THOUGHT AND BEHAVIOUR

RESTRICTED PLAY

Although a few pupils with autism will acquire the rudiments of symbolic or pretend play, as we have seen, it is often very stereotyped and fails to develop in any creative way. In extreme cases of withdrawal, the pupil may prefer forms of vestibular or sensory stimulation to productive play with toys or materials. Such children may spend their time twirling or rocking or flicking their fingers or a bit of fluff into the corner of their eyes. They may even head bang or pick at their skin or pluck out their hair, or engage in other distressing forms of self-mutilation such as eye-poking.

Failure to engage in rich role-play situations is not only a reflection of the pupil's difficulties but also leads to further difficulties; the pupil misses valuable opportunities to take on the role of others, to act out emotions and events and to learn all the social and language skills that go with these activities. Such play should therefore be encouraged and aspects of it taught directly, although it is extremely difficult to engender spontaneously. Earlier chapters suggest how this might be approached through the use of greater self and other awareness. Thus, a failure to engage in play might increase social isolation and lead to a kind of sensory deprivation, or at least boredom. This in turn could lead to a range of self-stimulatory behaviours, some of which may be damaging to the health and wellbeing of the individuals, and therefore need to be 'managed' or even eliminated. Others, while not dangerous in themselves, may seriously interfere with learning and block further development and so they too will need management.

RIGID ROUTINES

Many pupils with autism will tolerate a complete change in their surroundings (staying somewhere new) but become very anxious and upset by even the smallest change in surroundings, activities or events that they 'expect' to stay the same. They may also develop set routines which it is seldom possible or desirable to completely eliminate, but the pupil can be taught to limit them so that they do not become uncontrollable and unduly disruptive of learning. Limitation can be achieved by giving the pupil a marked period when the routine may be engaged in and a structure that assists with any waiting. This might take the form of a written timetable with the 'routine' period clearly marked or, for the less able non-verbal child, this might be a large clock or timer, or pictures or objects of reference that indicate the tasks that are to be completed first before the routine (also marked on the sequence by a picture or object of reference) can be indulged in. To begin with, of course, this will need to be a very brief 'waiting' period.

Variations in routine can be effected by providing external representation of stages (e.g. a written set of steps, or pictures or objects) which can then be manipulated by changing one of the steps and thus allowing the pupil to predict and prepare for the change when the routine is acted out. For example, a pupil may become agitated if an established PE apparatus route is changed. By writing down each apparatus activity on separate cards, or producing pictures of them, the pupil can first sequence them in the familiar way and then have them sequenced in the new way so that the actual event in the gym is predicted and understood and the threat thereby reduced.

LACK OF CREATIVITY AND SPONTANEITY

There is a tendency in autism to learn set solutions to problems and apply them rigidly. Reflective awareness, as indicated in earlier chapters, will help with this as will being taught to express intentions and plan behaviour. To begin with teachers may need to impute these intentions because pupils may not be aware of their own. Pupils also need practice at making, and sticking with, genuine choices and they need to learn how to achieve the same goal through a range of different means. Failure to take account of these difficulties could lead to frustration and stress and subsequent undesirable behaviours.

When thinking of creativity, it is important to make the distinction between the 'means of creating' and a 'creative act'. This applies across the curriculum to areas such as making friends or eating a reasonable range of foods as well as to areas more generally regarded as 'creative'. We should not assume that the child has made a choice to be on his or her own or to eat only chips and custard (perhaps together) unless we know that the child has the ability to make and keep friends or has experienced a range of foodstuffs, in each case. In art, if the child always covers paper with black paint we cannot call it 'creative' if the child has no experience of using other colours and does not know how to draw representationally. Once we have taught all these skills and ensured all these experiences and the child persists in covering paper with black paint, we can then assume a creative choice.

SELF-DIRECTED INJURY, TANTRUMS, AGGRESSION

These behaviours may arise from boredom, under-stimulation or over-stimulation. There may even be direct biological causes. Most of this behaviour, however, is best treated as an immature method of communication. This means looking for the triggers of the behaviour in the environment, and taking account of the pupil's difficulties, in determining what is causing the behaviour and how it is being 'rewarded'. Once the communicative intent has been identified, the pupil can be taught an alternative way of expressing that intent, as was discussed in the chapter on communication. It is important here, however, to reiterate the distinction between imposing one's will on a child and teaching a better way to communicate an unwillingness to co-operate. Both teaching goals are valid; it is a matter of teacher judgement as to which one takes priority in any teaching situation.

Other ways of reducing unwanted behaviours might be to examine the environment and the pupil's situation. Teachers need to ask if the pupil is in pain, or thirsty or hungry. They need to look to ways of better structuring the environment so that the pupil knows where to go and what to do at all times. They need to question if there is an adequate way of warning the pupil about imminent change and whether or not the pupil can predict the sequence of events and know when there will be free time or the return of a favourite object or activity.

If all detective work on the environment fails, it may be sensible to look at the pupil's physiological state and perhaps introduce a period of vigorous exercise to regulate the body chemistry. Pupils with autism may not choose to take physical exercise in the same way that they may not choose to do lots of other things, but that does not mean that they do not need it.

DIFFICULTIES WITH INTERFERING BEHAVIOUR

CLASSROOM CONTROL

There is not only the problem of controlling the behaviour of the pupil with autism so that it does not disrupt the learning of the other pupils, but also the problem of double standards when monitoring behaviour. It may not be in the interest of the pupil with autism to be forced to participate in certain social situations or to cope with assemblies but it may be difficult for others to understand why he or she can 'get away with it'. It is also worth remembering that pupils with Asperger's syndrome in particular often find it hard to be 'picked out' in any way and thus resist commands directed at them explicitly. However, if the command can be rephrased as a general rule, this difficulty is overcome.

Some of these problems can be eased by developing a system of discipline that is explicit and will have benefits for all the pupils. This means that rules for behaviour and consequences of infringement are clearly established and made known in a form that the pupils can understand. For mainstream pupils (including those with autism, able enough to be educated within this setting) this may involve written rules displayed where all can see. For those with moderate learning difficulties or young mainstream pupils, the rules may be spoken and key relevant rules for particular lessons emphasised at the start of the lesson. This might be supported by pictures or symbols displayed as a reminder of the rules. Those with severe learning difficulties might work towards the spoken rules with picture and symbol backing, while those with profound learning difficulties would need to have the rules established by emphatic practice. Thus the consequences of behaviour would need to be salient to the pupils concerned and consistent and immediately contingent, if the connection with the behaviour is to be made.

One of the advantages of developing explicit 'discipline' systems in this way is that it forces us to question the value, justice, and ultimately the necessity of many of the school or classroom rules with which we operate. If there are rules that are difficult for the child with autism to understand and follow, it may be that we need to adjust the child, but more often we find it is easier and better for everyone if we adjust the rule. Of course, there will be rules of safety and concern for others that we cannot relax and would want to teach to children with autism for their long-term benefit. But it can be very liberating for all if we can jettison some of our petty rules, while emphasising and enforcing the important ones, giving all pupils a greater sense of responsibility for their own actions, in the process.

DEVIANT COGNITIVE SKILLS

The able pupil with autism may well have a particular 'islet of ability' (often connected with an area of specific interest). For all pupils with autism, regardless of general ability, the acquisition of skills may be patchy so that skill in one area does not imply that other more basic skills have already been acquired. These features of autistic thinking require that we probe for understanding of apparent areas of knowledge or skill and are wary of teaching in traditional skill hierarchies (herein are problems with the National Curriculum). For example, we have already noted that a pupil with autism may find it a lot easier to learn to 'read' print than to retell a heard story.

INABILITY TO MAKE CHOICES

This can be at the most basic level with pupils not being able to select a meal from the dining room or decide whether or not they want milk today, or it may be at the level of not coping with unstructured situations such as 'free-choice' periods.

It is comparatively easy to teach a child to go through the motions of making choices, but, without understanding, it is very difficult to get pupils to make meaningful choices. As an example, one of the authors once tried to teach a 14-year-old girl with autism and severe learning difficulties to indicate a choice by signing 'yes' when offered something she wanted and 'no' when offered something she did not want. The impetus for this programme was that she hated puddings and, when offered one by an unsuspecting dinner lady she would go berserk, screaming and biting her hand and often throwing the offending item. The teaching plan seemed straightforward. The girl would be offered a pudding and immediately prompted to sign 'no'. The pudding would then be removed and she would be offered a piece of fruit (which she loved) and prompted to sign 'yes' before being given it. In each case the offer would be accompanied by the signed query 'Do you want this?' After a while the prompts would be faded. The order in which fruit or pudding were offered would be varied. The girl's preferences were so marked with respect to the pudding and the fruit that we felt she would soon learn this way of rejecting what she did not want. It should be remembered, however, that this girl was 14 and had a history of difficult behaviour which had been replaced over the years with largely compliant behaviour as she accepted the routines of school life. It was only her apparent revulsion to puddings that remained a trigger for violent assertiveness.

What in fact happened was rather different and very salutary when it comes to thinking of how to teach choice to someone who does not understand the concept. Everything went according to plan while rejection and acceptance were being prompted; there were no tantrums and the correct responses were given even when the prompts were reduced to a minimum. But the time came when the prompts were faded completely. The first few trials went well (there could only be one trial a day because of the nature of what was being taught) but then came the day when the girl made a mistake. She was offered a pudding and signed 'yes' instead of 'no'. Clearly, learning about the meaning of 'yes' required that she be given the pudding and staff waited for the expected outburst, ready to intervene with the prompted 'no' and then to offer the fruit. But there was no outburst. The girl took the pudding and ate it. The programme had worked in terms of getting rid of the tantrum but at the expense of choice. Presumably, in her mind, this was just another thing you had to do at school, in a long line of meaningless things, and she merely accepted it. The salutary part is that ever after she accepted and ate puddings. So there was an accompanying reduction in her quality of life as she went from the healthy preference for fruit to a liking for sweet puddings.

COMMUNICATION OF NEEDS, FRUSTRATION

It seems easier somehow to understand when and why pupils with autism and additional learning difficulties might become frustrated at not being able to communicate their needs. Certainly parents of children who do not speak often feel that frustration would be eased if only their child could tell them what was wrong or what was wanted. Yet, in spite of good linguistic skills, pupils with Asperger's syndrome also have problems of frustration. They may not understand the need to tell people what they want or what is troubling them; after all, they do not understand that others do not know what they know or feel. Thus they need to be shown how to do this, not only for their own well-being and development but also to prevent the flare-ups that often come when they are frustrated. They also need to be taught self-advocacy skills and how to resist bullying or abuse.

The obvious way forward is to teach children to respond to their own sense of unease or discomfort but, as we have already seen, children with autism will not have a sense of their own mental states and the consequence is that they are very vulnerable to all forms of abuse. This would not matter so much if they were equally impervious to the pain, but sadly this is not so. Indeed the distress of being bullied or abused may be made worse by the fact that they do not understand what is going on and cannot share their distress with anyone.

Equally, teachers and carers are vulnerable to accusations of abuse from diligent professionals who do not understand about autism and so may misunderstand what they see or hear. The child who has a precocious knowledge of sex terms, for example, may have acquired this as he or she might acquire all the technical names of rocks, or types of carrot. It does not imply, as it might with other children, that he or she has been exposed to sexual abuse of any kind. Equally, the child who masturbates until his or her sexual organs are sore, and who sticks objects into all orifices, may present a clinical picture of an abused child. If they are then asked whether a teacher or parent has ever touched them 'there', they are liable to answer truthfully and literally 'yes', not realising the implications that will be drawn, and not thinking to add that it was to soothe the soreness with cream, or whatever.

We have known instances where it was purely fortuitous that a teacher could disprove what a child with autism was apparently saying, or they might well have faced appalling consequences. An example was a child who told her mother that she had not been allowed to take part in a pageant (for which the mother had made a costume, and therefore was not best pleased) and had been forced to eat green jelly until she was sick. Some months later, at a parents' evening, a video of the pageant showed the girl in question happily in her pageant attire, scoffing green jelly so greedily that a teacher said to her: 'You had better stop eating that jelly Amy, or you will be sick all over your lovely dress and then you won't be able to take part in the pageant'. The mother, who luckily had not reported the incident but had told other parents, then admitted what her child had said and explained that she had believed her because she understood that individuals with autism do not lie. That is true, in the sense that they do not lie to deceive (although they may learn to lie to get out of trouble, since they can do that through predicting the consequence of behaviour without any understanding of mental states) but they are very likely, as in this case, to misunderstand and therefore, to misrepresent. The child's difficulties with telling the gist of an event meant that, when her mother asked her about the pageant, this just triggered the exact memory of what the teacher had said and so she gave that without any indication that it was a spoken prediction of what *might* happen rather than a description of what *did*.

PERCEPTUAL AND ATTENTIONAL PROBLEMS

There may be aspects of the environment that the pupil with autism finds difficult to ignore and which could trigger unwanted behaviours. Equally, the idiosyncratic perception and 'tunnel attention' of these pupils may make it difficult for them to see things in the same way as others, to understand which things 'go together' perceptually and to attend to the same meanings as others. They may also have particular sensitivities or be unable to 'foreground' information (such as the human voice) against meaningless 'noise', whether of a visual or auditory kind. This can make it difficult for them to pick out instructions against a background of classroom noise and the teacher should be aware of this and not automatically assume disobedience.

PROBLEM BEHAVIOUR AS A FORM OF COMMUNICATION

FRUSTRATED COMMUNICATION NEEDS

Underlying problems with communication often lead to behaviour problems. There are three basic needs that seek expression and that lead to difficulties if the individual has no way of doing this:

- to be given something
- to have something removed
- to have stimulation.

Problems in communication, therefore, mean these needs may be unmet, with resultant frustration. This in turn may lead to temper tantrums or to aggression or destructiveness. An interpretation of the actual causes then might be that the individual wants something altered, or is bored and unoccupied, or is attention seeking, or has a phobic reaction.

IDENTIFYING THE CAUSE

Generally, it is impossible to suppress disruptive behaviour without providing the individual with alternatives. Increasing communication skills usually leads to a decrease in disruptive behaviour. Treatment programmes might need to establish control as a priority, but the long-term approach should concentrate on building communicative alternatives. Whatever programme is adopted needs to offer structure and reassurance and needs to be applied consistently. As a first step, therefore, it is worth doing a functional analysis of the behaviour to suggest some hypotheses about causes and thus the communicative intent that it is useful to impute.

The first question to decide is to whom is this a problem? It may be that there is nothing in the behaviour itself that would merit its removal or suppression, but that there is just one individual who cannot tolerate it. Children with autism can have an uncanny knack of finding the one person who cannot bear to be spat at or whatever, if they want a maximum effect. If it is only one individual, it may be simpler to try to change that individual's behaviour or to remove them from the situation than to change the behaviour of the child with autism. It is only when we are asked to change our own behaviour, of course, that we realise how difficult that is and how resistant we are to doing so (this applies even where we recognise the need for change and want to do so as in giving up smoking or in dieting).

We also need to select an appropriate descriptor for the behaviour. For example, is it really aggression, or just a natural response to provocation? The behaviour should be described in terms of what the individual does (e.g. hits other with flat hand—there is a need here to be explicit and say who was hit, and how, rather than just 'disturbs others'). It is also important to note how often the behaviour occurs as this helps to identify any pattern and offers clues to possible triggers. In the case of behaviours such as temper tantrums or crying it is also important to note the duration of the behaviour.

It is necessary to look for the antecedents of the behaviour, to ask when it occurs and under what conditions. The kind of checklist given below should enable the teacher to develop and test hypotheses on triggers:

- Look for the time of day and think about this in terms of whether the child might be tired or hungry.
- Note which part of the lesson or activity it occurs in and think about whether the child might be bored.
- Examine the nature of the task and investigate hypotheses about whether the child might be expressing fear of failure, reacting to frustration, showing a lack of comprehension, or, once more, just being bored.
- Note who is present (staff, other pupils and so on) and look for an association with one of these or with the presence of someone new, or even the absence of someone familiar who 'should' be there.

We need also to look at the incident immediately preceding the behaviour, for example:

- Was the child approached by someone?
- Was the child told off, or were words used that might be interpreted as such?
- Had the child just been given a task?
- Had he or she just been directed by the teacher or by someone else (even another child)?
- Had the child just been teased by peers, either consciously or unconsciously?
- Was there a particular noise?

Then, of course, there is a need to consider the consequences of the behaviour. There is a need to look for attention from staff and/or pupils even if it is meant to be punishing (shouting, for example). Punishments (like rewards) are defined by their effects, not by the intentions of the person using them. Thus, if they are applied properly and do not lessen the behaviour then they are not punishers for that behaviour, in that individual, at that time.

TEACHING AN ALTERNATIVE FORM OF COMMUNICATION

Once the functional analysis is complete and it has been decided what it is that the particular problem behaviour is communicating, or, alternatively, what communicative act could sensibly be imputed to the non-communicating child, then that child can be taught an alternative form of communication to achieve the same ends. It is important to remember, however, that it is the communication that is the teaching aim and not anything else. For example, suppose that a functional analysis shows that what the temper tantrum 'means' in this particular case is that the pupil does not want to do the task set. The first step is to work out priorities for the pupil; is it more important that he or she does the task or that he or she learns a 'better' way of communicating the fact that he or she does not want to do the task? Assuming the answer is the latter, then the teacher must forget all notions of 'winning' and 'not letting the pupil get away with it' in favour of teaching the pupil to communicate his or her choice.

The teacher also needs to remember that in times of stress the pupil may not have his or her most sophisticated form of language available. It might be better to teach the pupil to push the adult away (gently) rather than to get him or her to say 'Please take this away' even if, under non-stressed conditions, the pupil would be capable of such a language structure. Of course, once the communicative gesture has been established and the pupil can trust the adult to take the task away (albeit only for a short while) when he or she indicates that that is what is wanted, then the teacher can gradually insist that a very little of the task is tackled before responding to the pupil's request. But the paramount step must be teaching the pupil to communicate his or her need directly with intent, rather than through the opaque message of a temper tantrum.

Thus, the procedure for teaching an alternative form of communication in this case might be as follows:

- Present the pupil with the triggering stimulus for the tantrum (in this case, the task).
- Immediately (i.e. before the pupil has a chance to begin the tantrum) physically prompt the pupil to push the task away gently, at the same time saying 'Oh! You don't want to do this. I see'. Remove the task and walk away.
- After a short interval (1 or 2 minutes depending on the situation) return the task and repeat Step 2.
- Continue repeating Steps 1, 2 and 3 for as often as possible on this occasion and then on other occasions, gradually fading the physical prompt in Step 2 until the pupil is pushing the task away spontaneously without signs of a tantrum or any stress.
- Now introduce another way of indicating that the task should be removed that is in line with the pupil's level of language ability. For example, a linguistically able child might be taught to say 'I don't want to do that now' or 'Please take this away'. A mute child might be taught to sign or gesture to indicate removal of the task. There should be considerable practice of using the newly taught form by repeating Steps 1 and 3 and allowing the new form of communication to take the place of Step 2.
- Once it is clear from the pupils' demeanour that they understand the communicative function of whatever form is being used, in the sense that they trust the teacher to remove the offending task whenever that form is used, the teacher should begin to negotiate about the task. When a child makes the communicative gesture or utters the phrase, the teacher should say something like, 'I understand that you don't want to do this and I will take it away in just a moment but do this little bit first'. Or the more able child might be shown a clock and told that the task will be removed when a certain time is up. It is important that the task requirements are minimal at this stage and do not disrupt the pupil's understanding of the effectiveness of the communicative gesture. For example, just get the pupil to fit one peg into a board or to do the task for 30 seconds only, at first. In time this negotiated period spent on the task can be lengthened gradually, always with the understanding that the pupil's communication will ultimately be respected, for that is, in this case, the priority teaching goal.

SHORT-TERM CONTROL STRATEGIES

As we shall see, there are particular reasons why a punitive approach is not appropriate in educating pupils with autism, even if there were not sufficient general educational reasons for this being the case. Nevertheless, in ideal settings and with the most skilled of teachers, there may still be occasions when some children with autism exhibit disturbed and disturbing behaviours which need to be dealt with for the safety of the individuals themselves as well as that of peers and staff.

None of us behave well all the time, with far less excuse than children with autism. Of course the temper tantrum of a two year old who is confused and angry and has not yet developed the social skills for more sophisticated responses, is generally accepted. Exactly the same frustrations and lack of social competence may underlie the behavioural outburst of the adolescent with autism, but we find it harder to make that connection because it is difficult to understand the depth of the social and communicative disability in someone whose other skills may be so much in advance of those of the two year old. Sheer size and strength is another major difference between the outbursts of the two. And the adolescent with autism will have no conscience and therefore no inhibitions about lashing out and attacking others. The combined result is that such an outburst can be very frightening for all who witness it, staff and peers alike.

There are two consequences of this. One is that staff need short-term strategies that manage behaviour effectively and keep everyone safe, while long-term strategies are being developed (or to cover the failures in long-term strategies that will inevitably occur from time to time). If this is not done, staff will remain fearful, the child might be avoided rather than educated and there will be little chance of any effective long-term strategies being put into operation. The second consequence is that staff may gravitate to short-term strategies that appear to be effective at the time but, as we shall see, could increase problems in the long term.

The explication of strategies for holding a child safely or restraining a child's aggression are not appropriately dealt with here. Such strategies need to be learnt in a practical context and practised regularly so that they can be used automatically and without panic at the appropriate time. It is essential that schools or care establishments have a whole-school (or whole-institution) policy which has been approved by parents, governors, and relevant professionals such as psychiatrists or psychologists. There is nothing to be gained from hiding one's head in the sand about such matters; that is where underhand and abusive practices emerge. An open and trusted policy that supports the staff and provides for the safety and care of all the pupils must be in everyone's interests. Of course, such a policy should be recognised as a short-term and emergency policy only and it should be run alongside a positive intervention policy aimed at reducing stress and the consequent occurrence of unwanted behaviour.

THE VICIOUS CYCLE

Imagine a typical classroom scenario, where a child with autism does something upsetting such as biting or kicking another child or beginning a high-pitched wailing. The teacher has not had time to observe the child closely, does not know what the immediate trigger was and has not made any systematic observations that could lead to hypotheses about general setting conditions as a possible cause. The teacher's effectiveness in this situation, then, will depend on the consequences of the behaviour. There are some consequences beyond the control of the teacher, arising directly from the performance of the act and its immediate effect on the child him/herself and on the other children. The teacher has a choice of four courses of action; he or she can:

- Add something unpleasant to the situation (in other words, punish the child directly).
- Remove something unpleasant from the situation (take away what it is presumed the child was objecting to, in other words, provide negative reinforcement).
- Add something pleasant to the situation (in other words, reward the child directly).
- Remove something pleasant from the situation (often assumed to be attention, or the company of others, but this is a doubtful assumption in autism. In other words, use a form of Time Out).

In practice there are problems with the use of punishment, which we will look at below. As far as the latter three strategies are concerned, the teacher often uses a combination of these and very often they work in the short term by stopping the unwanted behaviour. This then acts as a negative reinforcer of the teacher's actions (the actions have been followed by the removal of an unpleasant stimulus, the problem behaviour). Thus, faced with the same situation again, the teacher has an increased likelihood of using the same strategy.

But what is the child with autism learning? Taking the teacher's possible strategies in order (leaving punishment proper aside) we come to negative reinforcement. If the trigger for the bad behaviour is something to do with the work situation, it is very difficult for the teacher not to use such a strategy, at least in part. Thus, merely attending to the situation may often mean that work stops while the problem is dealt with. If the child enjoys fuss and attention, it is also difficult for the teacher to avoid the next strategy, rewarding the behaviour as he or she reacts to it.

The last strategy (Time Out) often fails in autism because what is assumed to be rewarding or pleasant is not so. For the child, removal from the teaching situation, or being made to face a blank wall, may of itself actually be rewarding. Thus, with each of the three strategies likely to be used by the teacher, the child may stop the unpleasant behaviour on this occasion because he/she has achieved his/her purpose; the unpleasant task has been removed, the child has received a lot of interesting stimulation with teacher going purple and shouting, and has been put in the peace and quiet of the hall away from the hubbub of the classroom which he/she found intolerable in the first place. Faced with the same situation again, the child too may have learnt what to do, and the vicious cycle is complete.

THE PROBLEM WITH PUNISHMENT

There are ethical problems with the use of punishment, of course, and it is becoming legally as well as morally indefensible in the UK at least. However, lest teachers think they are being deprived of an effective management tool, it is worth elaborating on some of the practical difficulties with punishment. The most telling objection is that it is ineffective in the long run. Even for the child without autism, there tends to be suppression of behaviour rather than its removal and the behaviour will reoccur the moment the situation changes in any way. The child does not learn not to jump on the settee, but not to jump on it when Daddy is around. There is then the problem that being in a situation where previously punished behaviours can be 'indulged' in without being punished may 'excuse' that behaviour and actually increase it. The child will jump on the settee more when Daddy is not around. This problem is exacerbated by the style of autistic learning and ways of remembering.

The use of punishment can also lead to unwanted side effects, such as fear, which is clearly counter-productive within an educational environment. There is also the problem that it may justify inflicting pain on others and what starts as an extreme reaction to extreme behaviour (using electric shocks to save the eyesight of a boy who is continually poking his eyes, as has been done) ends up being used far more widely as people get hooked on an apparent 'solution' that requires very little in the way of planning or resources (or care, of course). Painful punishments in particular are liable to elicit aggression towards the punishing agent and others and have generally disastrous long-term consequences.

Another significant disadvantage of the use of punishment, especially in autism, is that it indicates what the individual should *not* do, not what he or she *should* do. As we have seen, children with autism will be at a loss, unless they have been taught an alternative strategy and an awareness that they have it. Since it does nothing to increase either the child's understanding or self-control it is also likely to replace one undesirable response with another and there is no guarantee that the next one will not be worse.

The key to a positive approach to behaviour management is the changing of the circumstances leading to the undesirable behaviour. The idea is to prevent, rather than deal with, such behaviour. Some approaches have tried satiation of the undesirable behaviour, where, for example, the child is made to tear and tear paper until (in theory) the child is sick of tearing paper and leaves the posters on the walls alone. Our experience is that this seldom works in practice with children with autism as a long-term strategy, but that the idea of ordering someone do the thing you do not want them to do can be effective in the short term. This may seem like negativism, but we think it is more to do with taking control and breaking the automaticity of the behaviour.

Ignoring the behaviour (Time Out) is fraught with difficulties. It can only work if we are sure there are positive rewards in the situation that we can remove effectively and, in the case of ignoring, that attention is one of them. This is not likely to be the case in autism. Even then, it will only work if we are sure the children cannot escalate their actions to the point where we have to pay attention. In that case all we will have done is to teach the child that throwing toys around the room is no longer enough to get teacher's attention, you now have to pick up the table and hit a vulnerable child in a wheelchair with it (this is an actual example that happened where an inexperienced teacher stuck rigidly to a programme devised by a rather rigid clinical psychologist).

The short-term strategy with the most likelihood of success in autism is the reinforcement of incompatible behaviour. Here the child is taught to do something else in the situation that presumably serves the same purpose and provides the same satisfaction, and is impossible to perform at the same time as the unwanted behaviour. Unless we do this, as we discussed in the chapter on emotional development, we are often in effect denying the child the expression of a legitimate emotion. We want more emotional expression, rather than less, so it is important that we give children a safe outlet for their feelings. An able boy with autism in a mixed setting had developed a habit of kicking hard whenever he was frustrated. Clearly, this interfered with lots of other educational aims (such as getting him to have friends) but attempts to get him to stop by kicking a ball instead or sitting on a cushion were unsuccessful. Neither activity, it seemed, replaced the satisfaction of a heavy shoe on someone's shin and the exciting responses that it generated. Giving the child a cap from a toy pistol, however, and getting him to stamp his foot (with the explosion as a bonus) did do the trick. There was a slight problem in that he then wanted to stamp on caps at times other than when he was angry, but the novelty wore off and he eventually accepted foot stamping as an alternative to kicking others, without needing the cap.

It is a fact of classroom life that bad behaviour gets noticed and good behaviour is ignored. Behavioural control means reversing these contingencies and in particular rewarding behaviour that it would be impossible to perform at the same time as the unwanted behaviour. It may be possible to ignore any unwanted behaviour while the alternative is being built up, but if the behaviour is very disruptive it might be better to prevent it while physically prompting the alternative.

A POSITIVE APPROACH TO BEHAVIOUR MANAGEMENT

DEVELOPING POSITIVE REINFORCERS

The thrust of this book is a cognitive approach to autism and, as we have explained, we feel that only that kind of approach can really affect the way children learn and think (as opposed to perform). We would argue, therefore, that the important route to developing more appropriate behaviours lies in increasing children's understanding of the world and themselves as operators in it. On the road·to that development, however, there will be a need to affect immediate performance and so the issue of how to reinforce behaviour positively is a complementary one.

Responsiveness to reinforcers can be seen as forming a hierarchy, according to the general developmental level of the child. Many children with autism, because of the specific nature of their difficulties, will be functioning only at the earliest levels of this hierarchy. The hierarchy can be described as follows:

- *Primary*—related to physical needs and sensations. It is common to find children with autism, even with advanced academic skills, who still respond only to reinforcers at this level. The child who is responding only at this level does not have to be fed food or drinks but may be played music or given some form of vibratory massage or vestibular stimulation (twirling, swinging, rocking), both of which can be used to extend social contact with others.
- *Secondary*—from conditioning, e.g. money, praise (both generalised reinforcers). This can be extended from primary reinforcement by providing a kind of token system (either with actual tokens or stars or with ticks and points) which gains secondary status as a reinforcer at this direct level by being exchanged for these more tangible rewards.
- *Intrinsic*—arising from the performance, e.g. self-esteem. Clearly, a cognitive approach would have this level of responsiveness to reinforcement as its goal. The problems of achieving this in autism have been raised throughout the book.
- *Postponed gratification*—mediated by formulated long-term goals, e.g. academic award. This level of reinforcement is not available to many with autism. However, it is part of the aims of a cognitive approach and should be helped by many of the strategies suggested within that approach.

Moving the child with autism up this hierarchy of responsiveness will do much to ensure that reinforcers for appropriate behaviour can be made available in the naturalistic environment, This, of itself, may help to avoid some disruptive behaviour and will do much to improve the general quality of life.

AVOIDING UNWANTED RESPONSES

Often the best strategy is to look for cues to pre-empt or avoid trouble and to make sure the individual has sufficient communication skills and an appropriately receptive communication environment. The teacher needs to remember that the individual with autism is likely to be highly stressed by ordinary everyday events and the environment needs to be as stress-free as possible. The teacher also needs to remember that behaviour problems often start in a mild form, maybe as the result of some 'understandable' event such as toothache or an accidental scratch causing aggression. Over time, such behaviour not only gets reinforced in that situation but becomes part of the individual's repertoire of responses and the original cause may be replaced by other ones.

A summary of some of the steps to take to avoid undesirable behaviour might be:

- Ensure the child is free from physical discomfort.
- Avoid confrontational styles that provoke unwanted responses.
- Make sure the child knows some acceptable way of responding to the situation and how he or she feels.
- Make sure the child knows an acceptable way of communicating his or her needs and trusts that communication to be understood and accepted.
- Ensure that there is a structure in the situation that tells the child what to do when, where, how and what is going to happen next (or ensure that the child is able to function without that structure).
- Make sure that instructions given (or language used) to the child are capable of being understood and are not a source of stress or confusion.
- Make sure that there are no stimuli which are unpleasant for the child or, if these are unavoidable, that the child has some known way of controlling the stimulus or its effect (such as headphones to block out noises).
- Check that there are sufficient accessible positive reinforcers in the situation for the alternative behaviour you want to encourage, to be maintained.

Even where these aspects of providing a positive environment are specific to autism, this kind of approach is likely to produce a more effective educational environment for any child.

CONCLUSION

Managing behaviours is a central issue in autism. But it is also a deceptive one. We may be seduced by short-term 'solutions' which subsequently create significant long-term problems. We may think of particular behaviours as inexplicable and intractable where, in fact, their genesis can be readily located in the autistic way of thinking and where there are readily available positive ways of dealing with them. Autism, then, requires that we rethink our conceptual understanding of notions such as 'challenging behaviours', 'classroom control' and 'reward and punishment'. For example, our notion of challenging behaviours needs to include withdrawn and isolated behaviours as much as aggressive or more obviously disturbing ones since these should all be a challenge to our teaching skills.

Curricular Issues

8

INTRODUCTION

In this chapter we deal with some particular curricular issues that are of special relevance in autism. It is beyond the scope of this book to deal with all aspects of the curriculum and we have chosen to focus where we think we can best illustrate the implications of a cognitive curriculum. That is not to say that we do not value other aspects.

WHEN TO START FORMALLY EDUCATING?

It is more effective to provide specialist input as early as possible, to enable future benefit from more integrated settings, wherever appropriate. This has implications for working with parents at the pre-school stage and for the actual provision made. Most parents would probably welcome early specialist provision, especially if allied to a policy of training the skills needed for later integration into mainstream settings. It might be more difficult to get all parents to see the advantages of early specialism followed by placement in a school for children with moderate or severe learning difficulties. Yet there are liable to be many children with autism who have additional learning difficulties and whose needs would not be appropriately met by mainstream schooling, given any foreseeable level of resourcing. Among this group will be some who will always need specialist input, but others who would benefit from being with children who do not suffer the same communication and social difficulties, but where their general academic learning needs could also be met appropriately. As with integration into mainstream schools, however, the benefits of such a placement are not automatic and the child with autism would need specialist input to develop the skills needed to learn from others and to work in groups. In the current climate, where specialist provision is fought for, the placement in non-specialist provision other than mainstream is liable to be seen as 'demotion' and professionals would need to work with parents in pursuing such a policy.

A policy of specialist pre-school provision would, thus, serve a number of needs.

- It would enable the identification and training of basic social and communication skills to enable later effective placement in non-specialist provision, whether mainstream or for more general special needs.
- It would support parents and families in the management and education of their child with autism so that problems might be avoided both in the child's development and in the possible social and human cost of family breakdown.
- It would support parents in their need to be doing something positive to help in the education and development of their child. This, in turn, would make parents less vulnerable to claims of the many peddlers of 'cures' for autism, while giving them a sound basis for optimism.
- It would enable education to be more adventurous and open. Free of the constraints of nationally set guidelines, education could follow unproven but hopeful avenues, especially where the programme uses extensive and intensive adult interventions that would be impossible to resource completely with professionals. Using parents and volunteers in such programmes is far easier at the pre-school stage than at other points in school life.
- It would provide research opportunities not only into the early development of children with autism, but also into effective teaching techniques.
- It would develop and spread the expertise in educating children with autism among parents and staff. Parental involvement would be a high priority for such a specialist service so that parenting skills were enhanced and parents were not de-skilled in any way.

WHERE TO EDUCATE?

INTEGRATION BY LOCATION

Because of the range of learning difficulties that can accompany autism, pupils with such difficulties may be found in a variety of educational settings, including mainstream. Yet autism offers a particular challenge in terms of integration into the mainstream because, as we have tried to show in this book, the autistic style of thinking and learning is so clearly distinct from the non-autistic. If there is to be integration in a mainstream setting then, as a necessary prerequisite for any progress, teachers and support workers need to make themselves as knowledgeable as possible about autism. Where this does not happen then there is likely to be a continuing misinterpretation of behaviours, language, and so on. The normal template for understanding other people does not necessarily apply in autism. Somebody who is a very good, intuitive teacher of non-autistic children will not necessarily be similarly successful with children with autism. In many ways, as our normal intuitions about what behaviours mean do not apply in autism, then we need to employ a kind of counter-intuitive thinking about the way in which we should approach the task and our relationship with the child.

COMMON AREAS OF DIFFICULTY IN INTEGRATION

If the child's time is spent in one-to-one sessions with a welfare assistant or support teacher, being helped to do the same tasks as the other children, or some 'watered down' version, then there will be little or no peer interaction. If no specific time is set aside for the child with autism to learn how to interact with his or her peers, and if those peers are not given any help in finding ways of interacting with the child, then he or she will effectively be 'segregated' with the adult. This effectively separates him or her from task-based interactions and any social interactions will be left for the playground. Ironically, task-based situations may be an easier social context for the pupil than the free ranging, fast moving social setting of the playground.

Tasks may well be reduced to a series of steps which give an illusion of commonalty (that the child is learning what everyone else in the classroom is learning) but which take little account of the child's special needs and the appropriateness of those tasks to meet those needs, nor of the meaningfulness of those tasks to the child. One of the authors observed a boy with autism fully integrated into a mainstream primary school during a period of 'sustained silent reading'. This was a boy who could read, at least mechanically, but no one had explained to him the process of silent reading and, of course, he only had overt behaviour to guide him. The teacher was happy with his 'involvement' in the task because he appeared to be doing what the others did, but that was, in fact, the difficulty. Close observation showed that he had learnt to select a book and then to watch others as a cue as to when to turn over the pages. He matched his overt behaviour exactly to that of his peers, but he missed the entire point of the exercise.

If there is not good communication between the class teacher and all the other professionals who may have some input into the education of the child (such as psychologists or therapists) then no connections can be made in terms of follow-up or reinforcement between what can become discrete areas of learning.

ACTIVE INVOLVEMENT OF THE CHILD

We do not suggest that all instances of 'integration' are negative. We know that there are cases where support is used sensitively in adapting the curriculum where necessary and, importantly, to manage opportunities for positive interaction between children with autism and their peers. But these things do not happen automatically simply by placing pupils in supposedly 'integrated' settings. Clearly, we need to move beyond regarding integration as relating merely to a setting and to recognise it as a process that needs the active involvement of the pupil. Warnock has already suggested three levels of integration: locational, social and functional.[6] We would add a fourth which would demand genuine adaptation of the curriculum and teaching approaches to meet the needs of the pupil with autism (though how far this is possible within the current UK national framework is a moot point).

SHORTCOMINGS OF SEGREGATION

In arguments for integration, the shortcomings of special education are always paraded. That seems to us to be a case for improving special education rather than abolishing it, especially where the alternative is at best unproven. Yet there may be features that are undesirable that are a direct result of the special segregated provision itself. Commonly these are taken to be effects on attitudes, and the later effects on 'normalisation'. There is some evidence that both teachers and normal peers increase their positive responses towards people with disabilities on exposure to them, but this is weighted in favour of those with physical, sensory or severe mental impairments. The evidence for groups such as those with autism is more equivocal. Certainly, mere exposure is insufficient, as was witnessed by a recent example where a boy with Asperger's syndrome was excluded from a mainstream primary school for 'bad' behaviour. The staff had been told of his 'condition' but not what it meant or how to help him. In such a situation, the diagnosis functions only as a label and can be used as an excuse for not meeting his needs ('We're not geared to deal with such children', as one key member of staff is reported as saying).

Efforts to 'reintegrate' pupils with autism into society after segregated education (through clubs, leisure, life skills, work, and so on) tend to be expensive and have not always proved very successful. Amongst many professionals there is a growing scepticism about the general rehabilitative effects of special institutions. This is certainly a danger, if the 'specialness' just means extra resources (which may be warranted, but will inevitably be at the expense of another child with special educational needs) without extra expertise. Parents and staff have a right to be critical of special education in the sense that they should subject it to critical analysis and examine the base for its claimed expertise. Nevertheless, good quality specialist education has been shown to make a significant difference to the future lives of those with autism, and we are convinced that it can be successful. It should be remembered that the ultimate goal is integration into society rather than integrated schools, and in some cases at least, this may best be achieved through early specialist education where the skills for later integration are taught. We also believe that the principle of normalisation means respect for individual differences, not ignoring them.

REVERSE INTEGRATION

One kind of integration which has claimed success with individuals with autism is 'reverse integration', where other children join the unit or class where the children with autism are normally located. Here, even if the full range of curricular subjects is covered, it is the normally developing children who are being 'integrated' into the special world of autism rather than fitting the traditional models of integration. This may have all sorts of long-term benefits for future integration into the community, if other people are to become more aware and better able to accommodate to the needs of individuals with autism. As mentioned in earlier chapters, playgroups that have taught the normally developing children how to play with those with autism have been particularly successful in increasing spontaneous play behaviour in children with autism.

INTEGRATED EDUCATION AND AN INTEGRATED SOCIETY

It is important to separate the goal of integrated education from that of an integrated society. We should not assume that integrated education is the only, or even the best, way to achieve an integrated society. There may be a requirement for a more flexible system that will allow periods of segregation and integration according to need at different times. It would be improper to state that children with autism should be in specialist educational establishments, or in partially or wholly integrated settings. Decisions on placement should be based on individual needs. What is clear is that children with autism require a special kind of teaching to match their special kind of learning; such teaching may be provided across a range of settings. It is not the place, but the quality of the education, that is important.

HOME AND THE CURRICULUM

A TWENTY-FOUR-HOUR CURRICULUM

There is clearly a need for parents to be involved in the education of children with autism and we discuss this in the section following this one. This need, of course, also applies to care staff where the child is in residential schooling or in some form of care provision, whether permanently or as respite. The need to argue for residential schooling, in particular, as an educational rather than a social need, has led to the notion of a 24-hour curriculum.

From the learning needs that have been described in this book, it will be apparent that education can neither stop nor start when the school bell rings. The nature of the learning difficulties are such that, in effect, the home or care situation is often a more natural and meaningful context for the education to take place, as many of the examples given in the book will illustrate. It is also clear that the education will only be effective if the strategies used are consistent across environments or, if there are appropriate differences, that these are made explicit so that discrimination can be taught. For the majority of pupils who live at home, then, involvement of parents will be vital for the success of the 24-hour curriculum.

PARTNERSHIP WITH PARENTS

It is important to involve parents of children with autism in their education for a number of reasons. There are the reasons that apply to all educational provision, about the value of home interest and support, about taking account of home and cultural values, and about learning more from those who know the child best and have a unique interest in the child's development. In addition, it is particularly important to involve the parents of children with autism because the nature of the children's difficulties pervades their development and these problems are not limited to academic concerns (indeed, they may be least apparent in academic areas). Parents are also likely to be under considerable strain in caring for their children with autism and will need (and seek) guidance from professionals about care and management issues. But again, in autism, there is a need for the teacher both to be particularly supportive of the parents in what can be a very bewildering and threatening situation and to work with the parents in quite specific ways towards an enabling of the all-round development of the child. We would agree with a tenet of the TEACCH programme, that 'children are best helped through and with their parents as co-therapists or collaborators with professionals'.[29]

There are, however, two notes of caution to be made. Parents of pupils with autism will often have had to face a tremendous battle in obtaining a diagnosis for their child and in obtaining appropriate educational provision. This, and the fact that training for professionals in autism has only recently begun, means that parents will often find themselves more knowledgeable about their child's condition than the professional whose guidance they seek. This can be a very threatening position for teachers to find themselves in and it reverses the normal power relationship between parents and professionals. Nevertheless, the principles of respecting equivalent expertise still apply, even if the balance or kind of expertise is different, and this should not be a barrier to effective partnership provided the professionals are not defensive and parents are realistic in their expectations.

The second note of caution is for teachers to recognise that their goals for the child are not automatically those of the parent. Pat Matthews, the father of a young man with autism, illustrated this with the metaphor that professionals were training for a sprint whereas parents were training for a marathon. It is parents who will have the continued involvement with the individual with autism well into adulthood and who cannot 'clock off' at the end of the day or week or even working life. In seeking to involve parents and work with them, teachers should make sure that the agenda set is a joint one and that 'partnership' does not just mean the parents supporting the teacher's goals.

EFFECTS OF AUTISM ON THE FAMILY

Many parents will arrive at the diagnosis of autism after a long battle to try to get some recognition of the particular difficulties faced by their child. Therefore there may well be a sense of relief at the actual diagnosis when it comes. But there is still likely to be some sense of guilt and/or anger in parents in the early stages of the child's life (indeed these feelings may persist). Mothers may doubt their 'mothering abilities' on the one hand and/or resent their child's lack of responsiveness on the other. Most parents will experience physical or psychological tension at some time and many parents report a feeling at some point or other that they need 'to escape'. Clearly, this kind of feeling puts additional strain on family relationships. Brothers and sisters are affected not only by the behaviour and problems of the sibling with autism but also by the resulting increased tension in the family.

At the time of adolescence parents often report a realisation that their child with autism will remain intellectually and socially a 'child in an adult's body'; many parents express great difficulty with decisions about what they interpret as 'institutionalisation'; there are commonly feelings of guilt and sadness and a feeling that the normal release from parental obligations will not occur. Thus families who may have weathered the storms of childhood and come to terms with their child's persisting difficulties may find that the feelings of guilt and anger resurface as they try to cope with the adulthood of their son or daughter with autism. It is at this point that siblings may become more involved and this in itself can cause problems if parents feel uneasy about passing on the responsibility of parenting.

Of course, the other effect of having a child with autism is to enrich the life of individuals and of families. Despite all the difficulties many parents of our acquaintance would wish us to note here that the child is primarily their child and is cared for and loved as such, regardless of the autism. And many brothers and sisters would say that they are influenced in a positive way because of the autism, in some instances to the extent of choosing careers in the caring services and so on.

RESPONSE OF THE PROFESSIONS

Assessment should include a diagnostic history of the child's development, in order to give a full picture. While this is said with good reason, and while it is clear that parents are in an ideal position to help in this respect, at least in the early stages of schooling, there is also an inherent difficulty with retrospective interpretations of a child's development. It is possible for parents of children with autism to give plausible explanations as to how they themselves were at fault in relating to, and handling, their young child. This may in part be guilt but also results from the fact that early parent–child interactions, as we have shown, are two-way processes. They are in fact *trans*actions and necessarily require input from both parties (i.e. parent and child); for relationships to develop both have to elicit and to respond. In the case of a child with autism eliciting and responsive behaviours will be absent from what should be early parent–child interactions. Parents may perceive therefore, in retrospect, that their actions were 'faulty' (and of course they may be right in that it is impossible to create a transaction when your partner does not react appropriately), but the reasons stem from the inabilities of the child rather than inadequacies on the part of the mother or the father.

Clearly, the role of being a mother or father may be central to a person's sense of self-esteem and therefore implications of inadequacy in this respect will be particularly salient. And certainly, if the parent already has a low sense of self-esteem, then any 'newly acquired evidence' is likely to add justification to existing feelings of inadequacy. An important concern for the professional, therefore, should be to guide the parents to a greater understanding of the nature of autism and of the positive part that they can play in the social and intellectual development of their child. Whatever the state of the parents' self-esteem it is clear that anxiety and inadequacy are likely to be two initial reactions on the part of parents. In the study by the DeMyers it was noted that about half the mothers of children with autism 'partially blamed themselves for the onset of autism in a non-specific way'.[4]

Autism is a pervasive developmental disorder and this pervasiveness means that it can only be effectively addressed if work is carried out across the range of the child's experiences. Also, it is clear that the difficulty in generalising is central to the condition; again therefore, there is a need to deal with issues (such as toilet training) in consistent ways across the child's learning environments. And learning environments are not neatly circum-scribed by the school syllabus or even by the school day. Therefore it is essential that parents and teachers work together, perhaps in a way that is unique in terms of parent–teacher collaboration in the general population. Parents should be able to play a central role in mediating the child's basic difficulty in generalising learned skills from one place to another.

One aspect of this uniqueness is that parents, in matters of the education and care of their particular child, can be both apprentice *to*, and trainer *of*, the teacher. This is because to educate, and care for, children with autism well, one has to know them well, and parents have the potential to know about and understand their own children better than do teachers who may see a child very little in terms of his/her whole life. Parents are, then, in a unique position when it comes to identifying their child's particular difficulties and the events that act as triggers and the adult responses that effectively resolve them. And they know about what may be very idiosyncratic ways of encouraging desirable behaviours.

It is also clear that teachers and parents need to join together to advocate the social and educational needs of individuals with autism in a wider sense. It is noteworthy that as autism has been increasingly widely recognised over the last 60 years, in many countries, it has been parents who have been in the forefront of the struggle for recognition and for appropriate educational and social provision. Indeed, in some cases parents have been opposed by the very professionals who should be creating the relevant services. Clearly, this is unsatisfactory. There needs to be a collaboration in which both groups recognise and respect the interests and kinds of expertise of the other. Having said all the above, we should also recognise that many parents of children with autism may already be under considerable strain. It would not be right, then, for teachers to add to that burden by expecting total commitment and time spent on 'education'. There is a need for families to be just that and to get on with the rest of their lives.

HOMEWORK

The learning needs of pupils with autism need to be taken into account in the setting of homework, and there are many sources of misunderstandings in this area that can affect parent–professional relationships. Difficulties most commonly arise in mainstream secondary settings, especially where different subject teachers may not be aware of the potential for misunderstanding and may interpret confusion as disobedience or laziness. The teacher may not realise, for example, that the pupil may have to be told to memorise or listen in a direct way and may have to have homework specified much more clearly than for others since he or she may not realise or remember its connection with a lesson. The episodic cues associated with the setting of the homework must be known and available to the parent, or the parent will not be able to co-operate in seeing that the homework is completed. Teachers will need to give parents these (or write them down for the pupil) so they can be used in the home setting. They should also be aware that pupils with autism may have particular difficulty in accepting (and therefore reading) different handwriting, and that failure to follow a written instruction may result from that alone.

SANCTIONS

When gaining parental co-operation for sanctions, teachers should also be aware that pupils with autism may have particular difficulty in accepting certain punishments (e.g. written lines or detentions) when there is no awareness of having done something 'wrong' nor any social understanding of the 'purpose' of such activities. It is unfair to expect parents to impose or even agree to sanctions which are not acceptable to the child, even if they apply to others. This can be a problem where teachers are rigid and rules inflexible, but it does not help the child for teachers to behave as if they too had autism. The principle which could be fairly applied to all is that the sanctions are *seen* as fair by all pupils and then it is up to the teacher to help the pupil (and his or her parents) see the fairness of the procedure—another educational opportunity!

AUTISM AND THE NATIONAL CURRICULUM

ACCESSING THE NATIONAL CURRICULUM

Having earlier made a number of general points relating to the difficulty of adapting an inappropriate curriculum for use with children with autism we now include some comments that relate specifically to the UK National Curriculum. Readers should note that the Curriculum has recently been revised and is now much shortened, with a smaller compulsory element. It remains subject-based, even in its proposed revisions, but it may well be that the section below will need reinterpretation in the light of developments subsequent to the time of writing. Ways of accessing the National Curriculum are addressed in other documents (including the access documents published by the Inge Wakehurst Trust[14, 22]), but here we discuss some more general problematic issues.

CONTENT

We do not suggest that access to particular subjects should ever be denied to pupils with autism, on the grounds of the autism alone. As we have tried to show, certain subjects will have particular meanings for certain pupils, and may be of particular interest, even where they would not generally be thought to have much relevance. What we would argue, is that the choice of subject appropriateness should be that of the teacher (in consultation with parents and other professionals) who will be able to create priorities for learning according to individual needs and not to nationally set criteria.

- Personal and social education needs a higher priority than the non-assessed cross-curricular dimension that is suggested by the National Curriculum.
- The pupil's disruptive and obsessional behaviour and the need to teach social and communicative skills directly, all serve to limit curricular access to the full range of National Curriculum subjects.
- There is some doubt whether learning about certain aspects of subjects such as history, geography or a modern foreign language is really a curricular priority for a pupil whose bizarre behaviour and lack of social understanding is far more likely to lead to problems in adjustment to life later on than will any lack of academic qualifications.
- The deviant nature of development of these pupils means that there is seldom the progression through the levels of each attainment target as is suggested by the National Curriculum and any national assessment results may be misleading in terms of the learning and understanding that has been achieved (see the later section on assessment).

DELIVERY

The National Curriculum does not set ways of teaching, but the programmes of study often imply teaching approaches that will be problematic for pupils with autism.

- The teacher will need to structure tasks more effectively than is suggested by the programmes of study.
- Teaching conditions will need to allow for the replacement of much of the group collaborative learning tasks by one-to-one sessions with a teaching adult or by access to appropriate software on a computer.
- Verbal comprehension, even in the apparently verbally able, may not be very good and there may be confusion over the meaning of certain terms and the giving of verbal instructions. Alternative methods of presentation (written instructions, diagrams, physical guidance) may be better suited to some pupils or some kinds of learning.
- Many individuals with autism appear to have their own culture (in the sense that they derive their own meanings from events without reference to others) and to be alien to our culture. Teaching should respect this cultural difference and try to ensure that activities have meaning for the pupils in their own terms.
- For similar reasons it is often better to use factual material as a basis for acquiring skills and knowledge rather than causing confusion with fiction. However, there may be reasons, to do with joining in class events and learning to appreciate 'our' culture, why fictional stories should be taught in spite of the difficulties.
- On the basis of a child-centred approach as one more likely to achieve

worthwhile learning, the pupils' special interests and abilities should be capitalised on throughout the curriculum.

- The curriculum for pupils with autism should not just be about acquiring 'bits' of knowledge or learning compensatory functional skills; it is essential to try to produce more effective learners and individuals who can think for themselves, as far as possible. This can be approached by teaching through a process of reflection (as discussed throughout the book) in a way that permeates all subject areas.

SPECIFIC SUBJECT DIFFICULTIES

The following are by no means comprehensive or, conversely, applicable to all pupils with autism, but they offer guidelines of the kind of difficulties that teachers may encounter.

- *PE*. Difficulties in gross motor co-ordination may lead to fear of heights and being unable to jump over obstacles, skip or catch and throw a ball underarm. Social problems may lead to difficulties with team games.
- *History*. Reciting and memorising lists of kings and queens or dates may be relatively simple for the more able pupil with autism, but there is greater difficulty when it comes to using empathy as a way through to understanding the human experience of different peoples at different points in time.
- *English*. There may be problems with fiction versus factual reading and writing as indicated above. Clumsiness or difficulty in initiating motor movements may also affect handwriting, and reading skills may outshine oral language ones.
- *Maths*. Number and some computational skills may be advanced but there is likely to be difficulty with estimation, and algebra. There is also the problem of generalisation, especially in relation to maths.
- *Modern Foreign Languages*. Provided the pupil has no difficulties with language learning (from specific or general learning difficulties), there may be no difficulties in acquiring the mechanical aspects of another language. However, the cultural variations in language use will exacerbate the individual's difficulties in understanding and using language in its social context and modern ways of teaching that concentrate on pragmatic aspects will disadvantage the pupil with autism, who would learn faster from a more traditional concentration on grammar and vocabulary.

ASSESSMENT ACROSS THE CURRICULUM

PROBLEMS WITH ASSESSMENT

One of the problems in applying any standardised assessment tests to individuals with autism is the fact that such tests often assume a normal developmental route in the acquisition of skills and knowledge. Autism, however, is characterised by deviance from this normal developmental pathway and therefore scoring on tests needs to ensure that the results are not misleading. Thus, many tests will suggest an entry point appropriate to the child's chronological age and, if the child scores at this level, all scores below that are automatically credited. If this procedure is adopted with individuals with autism, significant gaps in the achievement of the individual may well be missed and early skills (assumed to underpin later ones) should always be checked. The psycho-educational profile of skills (PEP) which forms part of the TEACCH curriculum[29] is extremely useful in this respect in that it identifies not only skills that have been mastered but also those that are emerging, and should provide a firm focus for teaching.

Formal assessment may also be misleading in autism if the test is carried out in a one-to-one situation, free from social distractions, with structured materials and clear unambiguous instructions. These conditions (whose very formality may be off-putting to the majority of children) will be ideally suited to maximise the performance of the child with autism. This is fine if what is wanted is a measure of optimum performance. If, however, the purpose of the assessment is to identify teaching goals or to gauge the effectiveness of teaching, then it is more important to know how the child functions in everyday situations with respect to the aspect being tested than to have some record of a notional 'ideal' level of achievement that is never reached in practice.

One-to-one sessions and formal tests may be useful to identify particular problems or to obtain a norm-related score that will enable comparisons with others for research or administrative reasons. But if the prime purpose is to obtain information on the individual's strengths and weaknesses for teaching purposes, then such formal assessments will need to be supplemented by observational assessments of functioning in everyday settings and/or by structured interviews or checklists filled in by those with ongoing daily contact with the child in the natural environment.

A third avenue for the possibility of obtaining misleading assessment information comes from the way many tests are constructed and the instructions used to get the individuals being tested to display their knowledge. A common format for language tests, for example, is the division of the test page into four pictures which provide contrasting alternatives for the form being tested. A vocabulary test at a simple level might have four pictures of different objects, or a test of grammatical understanding might have four pictures offering, for example, one picture of a dog under a bed, one of a dog on a bed, one of a dog beside a bed, and one of a dog in a bed to test for understanding of the preposition 'under'. In each case the child has to point to the correct picture following the instruction of the tester in respect to the item being assessed. For example, for testing 'under' as in the illustration above, the child would be told to 'Show me "the dog is under the bed"!'

It is in the use of this instruction that the potential confusion lies. Many children with autism will understand 'under' (ostensibly the term being tested) but will fail to respond correctly to the command because they do not understand the word 'show'. 'Show' is such a common word in instructions in language tests (even in the more informal kinds where the language therapist or teacher is testing for understanding of the labels of common everyday items) and is used so early in communicative exchanges with babies, that adults (even language professionals) seldom recognise that its meaning is rooted in an understanding of communication. If you do not understand about communication, then you will not understand what 'show' means or how to go about 'showing' someone something.

Of course, extensive prompting and practice with this kind of activity can give individuals with autism an understanding of what is meant by 'show' but that understanding tends to relate to the particular test situation only. Initial testing using this instruction may lead the tester to conclude that the individual has not understood the form being tested whereas the lack of understanding lies elsewhere. It is useful for teachers to teach individuals the meaning of words like 'show' but testing does not need to wait for such knowledge to be acquired. It may violate the strict standard-isation procedures for validating a test, but for most common purposes the instructions can be altered to avoid the use of 'show' by substituting 'Point to . . . ' or even 'Put your hand on . . . '. Once the individual is given an instruction that is understood then it becomes possible to fulfil the purposes of the test in testing the understanding of the particular forms it was designed to examine.

ASSESSING COMMUNICATION

There are language scales that have pre-verbal communication sections and there is a tendency for communication to be assessed only as a non-verbal precursor to language development. Yet there is a need for communication to be assessed, regardless of the individual's level of language ability. Structured observations across a number of situations will provide a context for such assessments but it is important to remember the contextual basis of much of the learning of individuals with autism and that behaviour that is present or absent in one setting gives no indication of its presence or absence in another.

When observing children with adults who know them well, the observer should take care to note the extent to which the communication is being structured by the familiar adult and to be aware that the child might only be able to function at this communicative level because of that support. This is also a factor to be wary of when using checklists that require information from key workers or parents. Very often these individuals will be unaware of how far they have adjusted their way of interacting with the individual with autism to provide the level of support necessary to sustain the communication; they may thus attribute communication skills to the individual with autism that are in reality mere reactions to the prompts and cues provided.

The ethnographic method uses a qualitative assessment of naturalistic observations in which the interactions are as important as what the individual being assessed actually does. It is through the reactions of others, and that individual's reactions to others, that a true picture of the individual's understanding and ability emerges. Description of this methodology can be found in texts such as the chapter in *School Discourse Problems* by Ripich and Spinelli.[27]

Alternatively there are checklists that can be used. Here we give just three representative examples. (1) *The Pre-Verbal Communication Schedule* (PVC)[18] is, as its name suggests, geared towards pre-verbal communication but it is useful for assessing communication in autism (especially in less able individuals) in that it was trialled on such individuals and it includes negative as well as pro-social forms of communication. (2) *The Pragmatics Profile of Early Communication Skills*[7] is based on interview information gained from parents and other caregivers. It assesses the communicative functions used by the individual, the responses made to the communicative attempts of others, how the individual reacts to others generally and particularly in conversational situations and finally how the individual communicates in different contexts. (3) Checklists provided as part of the TEACCH Communication Programme[32] cover assessment in five areas. Firstly *means* are assessed (this involves assessing the child's capacity to use and understand the various modes of communication). *Vocabulary* is then assessed followed by *form*, i.e. the level of complexity achieved in whatever mode is being used. The number of communicative *functions* the individual has are then assessed. Finally *context* is assessed because behaviour that is found in one context may not be present in another.

ASSESSING SPECIFIC ACADEMIC AREAS

This book has not the space to deal with general issues in the assessment of specific subjects such as language or mathematics or to act as a guide for such assessment. In general, the methods and tools that are generally used for assessment in that subject will be applicable to those with autism, with the provisos mentioned above in the general section on assessment. The more difficult and unique area of assessing communication has been dealt with above. Social functioning may be assessed from observations and in particular from the ethnographic method given in the section on communication. There are also some standardised tests that may be used, such as the revised Vineland assessment,[8] that will enable norm-based comparisons to be made.

In spite of good and appropriate teaching, there are not only day-to-day fluctuations in performance, due to physical and psychological factors, but also in a minority of cases, apparent regression in that skills and knowledge are lost. Sometimes this is an artefact of the particular assessment conditions in that assessment at one period may differ from that at a later time, in that the skill was cued or prompted in some way or the person doing the assessment was more familiar with, and sensitive to, the child. Yet, sadly, loss of skills and knowledge has been documented in autism. This may follow a traumatic period, which might be the case for any child except that what counts as 'traumatic' may be very different for the child with autism. It may follow illness, especially if that involves a high fever, or it may follow a period of the rapid learning of new skills, which sometimes seems to lead to a loss of old ones unless these have been practised. It needs to be remembered that new skills and knowledge will not necessarily build on the old, unless the relationship is made explicit in the training of the new skill or the acquisition of the new piece of knowledge. Also, since most memories are cued, as we have seen, the learning of something new in association with the same cues will result in the replacement of the old by the new, unless the old is rehearsed as well.

Finally, there are conditions within the autistic spectrum, such as Rett's syndrome, where there is physiological and neurological deterioration over time which, sadly, often results in loss of function. In such cases, teaching has to be directed at maintaining current levels of functioning wherever possible, and finding new ways to enhance the quality of life with a deteriorating range of skills and abilities.

ASSESSING COGNITIVE ABILITY

The assessment of cognitive ability, and in particular the use of IQ tests in autism is controversial. Clearly, as the section on general assessment difficulties shows, there are problems that might lead either to lack of co-operation or to misleading results if the tester is not experienced in autism. However, IQ tests have been shown to be very reliable measures of cognitive ability in autism. There has even been some work with particular

IQ tests, identifying certain profiles of performance as characteristic of autism. Sometimes procedural changes need to be made to gain co-operation and understanding, but these are seldom severe enough to impair the usefulness of the test. We have found, for example, that test performance can be enhanced simply by giving the child an extra box to place unwanted items in, in solving a problem. Without this, the child is distracted by the fact that there is no place where these pieces 'belong' and spends fruitless time and effort trying to incorporate them into the solution. The most useful tests are often those devised for the non-verbal child which will frequently give a truer picture of potential, even for the child with spoken language ability. Of course, all these adjustments need to be noted, for they say a lot about the teaching conditions needed to effect learning, as well as assessment.

The controversy about the use of IQ tests, however, is concerned more with their validity than their reliability. Because of the patchy kind of performance that is typical of children with autism on IQ tests, any comparisons with other groups (as might be needed to get matched groups for some research project, for example) is best done on the particular subtests that are relevant to the comparisons being made. If global IQ scores were used, for example, the group with autism would be likely to be functioning at a much lower level of language ability than the comparison group and thus one would not know if any differences that were found were due to the autism or to this different level of language functioning. When it comes to information that will be useful in teaching, some global measure of IQ may give an indication of ability, but again, subtest scores are likely to be more helpful. What will also be important are notes on the process of taking the test for it is the reasons for failure (or indeed for success) that will give a much better guide to how the child is thinking and learning than a bare score.

PUPIL INVOLVEMENT IN MONITORING AND ASSESSING

INCREASED UNDERSTANDING OF SPECIFIC TASKS

Children with autism are likely to have a more complete understanding of a particular task subsequent to completing it if they have been involved in some way in the process of assessing it. One of the ways of increasing understanding may be to involve children in assessing the actual product that results from a lesson. In some cases this will occur naturally, as when the cake is eaten after the cookery lesson, but this will only be useful if its assessment function is made explicit (does it look/feel/taste nice?). Assessing the process that they went through when working on an activity is more difficult but involves even more opportunities for learning. For example, they can examine the ways in which they went about resolving problems in making the cake, any discussions they had, requests they had to make for materials and equipment, things they rejected as well as used, how easy or difficult certain stages were, whether the oven was at the right temperature, whether the butter and sugar were sufficiently creamed (did they change colour?), whether the eggs were added slowly enough (did the mixture curdle?) and so on.

In fact, of course, for the gain in children's understanding to be maximised then they need to be involved in assessing both the product, and the process. If they only assess the product then they are just engaging with their own learning at the surface level; they are assessing something which might have arisen from the process (of problem solving) that they went through, but which doesn't necessarily reflect all of the aspects of that process. By just looking at (or even tasting) the cake itself you may be missing, for example, the important decisions that were made about what to put in, and not put in, the finished article.

Teachers, then, need to aim to get children to question what they have learnt and the way in which they went about learning it. It may be that some high-functioning individuals with autism can use a structure of self-questioning after task completion that gets them to:

• Search for key points and key issues.
• State clearly (and so clarify) what they think they have learnt.
• Make explicit connections between what they have learnt and their prior knowledge in the same subject area.
• Make judgements about where/how their new learning will be useful to them in the future.

IMPROVING METACOGNITIVE ABILITY

As well as increasing understanding of particular tasks, self-assessment may have a more general positive effect on the thinking of children with autism. As we have already said, if we want to make pupils with autism more effective as learners, then one of the key things we need to do is to enable them to become aware that they can act in a problem-solving way and of how they have acted (in terms of their own ways of thinking and of learning). Clearly, being involved in assessing one's own work/progress draws attention to one's performance as a learner and so increases self-awareness in this respect.

Children with autism do not monitor their own thinking in the way that successful non-autistic thinkers do, and they therefore need a structure which enables them to do so. The structure would need to indicate to them the following facts at key points in any task: if they are right or wrong, when and how to check on their own understanding, when and how to make a judgement on progress and what criteria to use, and finally when to check that judgement against the teacher's. Clearly, as pupils become more successful then the structure can gradually be reduced and their performance carefully monitored to note whether or not they are able to self-monitor without it.

WAYS OF INCORPORATING SELF-ASSESSMENT INTO TEACHING/LEARNING PROGRAMMES

There are obviously levels at which self-assessment may take place. In a sense, all of these levels may have value for the teacher in some way, and all may have value for the learner with autism in some way. It seems useful here to summarise the levels because this may enable teachers to consider which kinds of self-assessments they are already using, what might be a step-up for particular children and what is possible for others. We start then with a fairly low level of pupil 'involvement' in self-assessment and work towards higher levels.

- Clearly, it is possible to involve children with autism in their own assessment by giving them some control over the checking or scoring. For example, giving them a maths 'answer book' and letting them check their own work, or giving them a picture of a tidy room so that they can know when tidying is complete.
- Making an assessment of progress (or product), based on criteria laid down by others. For example, doing a science experiment and checking at each stage that you have considered certain things (that materials and time are available, etc.) that have been set down by the teacher in advance.
- Using checking during a learning process to determine progress/success and feeding that assessment back into one's own learning. (The important distinction over the previous level being that the learner decides when and how to self-check, albeit from some set criteria.) An example might be in spelling—deciding when to check on spelling and which method to use. Of course, this could happen naturally, but it might need to be enhanced through specific training. In short, you get children with autism to test their own progress but you give them a clear structure within which to do it.
- Giving pupils responsibility for devising the criteria as well as carrying out an assessment using those criteria. So, for example, high-functioning children with autism might, at the start of an activity, decide on what qualities they should look for in a finished weather chart. Then they would assess their own finished piece of work using the criteria they themselves had defined at the outset.
- Involving pupils in making judgements about their progress, based on assessments made. Pupils with Asperger's syndrome might be encouraged to evaluate their own efforts in learning a foreign language, their use of

skills of translation and their progress as a learner (e.g. 'I think I am getting better at French pronunciation now that I have learnt to listen to the language tape more carefully'). An example of this kind of self-assessment would be the kind of Record of Achievement used in many secondary schools.

- Requiring pupils to make judgements that go beyond particular tasks and involve them as persons dealing with a range of activities/experiences and what they can do about it—i.e. using self-assessment to feedback into the processes of their learning in future situations. General reflective diaries are perhaps the best way of accessing this level of involvement in one's own learning.

CONCLUSION

We have tried to show in this chapter how autism requires us to reconsider the nature of a curriculum itself as well as the where, when and how of its delivery. The pervasiveness of the condition demands a special kind of all-embracing curriculum and affects everything we do within the curriculum including the way in which we try to monitor progress through assessment.

Entitlement to an Appropriate Education

9

INTRODUCTION

In this final chapter we consider the entitlement of children with autism to an education that meets their needs and then we summarise our own view of the form that education should take. Stanley Segal's claim in 1965 that no child is ineducable,[30] heralded a change that gave all children a right to education, framed in the 1970 Education Act.[5] In the UK we have moved from a situation where some children were hospitalised rather than educated and where special learning needs, where they were recognised, were assumed to be best met in segregated, specialist settings. We are now in a situation where the aims of education are supposed to be the same for all children, be they with or without autism, where we have a National Curriculum which is lauded as an entitlement for all, and where we have closed many of our specialist educational establishments in a vigorous move towards integration. Along the way from the first position to the latter a rhetoric has grown in which 'labels' have been depicted as unsavoury and unnecessary and normalisation has been highlighted as the key to integrated educational provision.

In our view some of the milestones along the route from the pre-1971 position to the present have been ill conceived, and the direction taken has been determined more by resource implications or by a particular ideological rhetoric than by a careful consideration of pedagogy. We would wish to separate out the current notion of entitlement to common educational aims related to content (which is what we have in the National Curriculum), from our own notion of entitlement to aims which derive from principles relating to the recognition and meeting of individual needs (which may vary between individuals and over time).

In practice, there seems to be growing, at least partial, acceptance of this view. Teachers are recognising the need for specialist training in providing appropriately for pupils with autism and greater control over in-service training budgets has led to increased interest in specialist training courses. An unwelcome corollary to this growing recognition of the special needs of pupils with autism, however, has been the publicity given to special programmes (often from other countries) that offer set methodologies for teaching pupils with autism. These are variable in quality and appropriateness, but our quarrel is not with any particular system or approach. Rather, we would contend that a set 'special' curriculum is just as inappropriate as a set common curriculum such as the National Curriculum. There may be good ideas or techniques that can be taken from such programmes, just as there are from the National Curriculum, but effective teaching must include judgements about curriculum content and teaching method that take into account individual differences (in pupil and teacher) and no 'recipe' approach can supply that.

THE NOTION OF ENTITLEMENT

If we assume for a moment that we as teachers think that the children with autism in our care are entitled to share a full, functional, age-appropriate curriculum with their peers, we need to ask of any educational situation that they are in, how effectively this can be achieved.

A BROAD AND BALANCED CURRICULUM

The breadth and balance of a curriculum depends as much on what is being received as on what is being delivered, and in this sense exposure does not equal experience. Just because a child with autism is sitting watching a sex education video does not mean that he or she is either receiving or making sense of the experience. Equally, we think it is important to develop strengths as well as trying to improve or remediate weaknesses, and there should be sufficient flexibility in the curriculum to be able to build on the child's interests and, where possible, use them in the remediation of any weaknesses. The breadth of the curriculum should be a meaningful breadth, judged over the span of school life; there is little point in forcing exposure to subjects where little can be gained whilst important curricular priorities, such as the building of social skills, are neglected. Teachers can be ingenious in teaching priority areas within subjects, but there comes a point when such practices are counter-productive and amount to tokenism.

A FUNCTIONAL CURRICULUM

This usually means 'preparation for independence' and, in a leavers' class containing pupils with autism, this is usually life skills. But are these aims functional for our pupils? For some they will be but, equally, some of the pupils with additional profound and multiple learning difficulties are not going to attain independent life skills. Rather, we suggest that functional needs for those children with autism may well relate to reduction in stress caused by social proximity, or reduction in self-mutilating behaviour, or to any of a long list of different and in most cases idiosyncratic needs. That is not to denigrate the teaching of life skills, but to redefine them to include as priorities the teaching of tolerance to the presence of others and the capacity to understand something of their social life and thus have a way of exercising choice within it. Ultimately, quality of life will be enhanced more by individuals becoming comfortable with others, so that others are comfortable with them, than by being able to half pull up socks that have had to be placed on their feet while they are kicking and spitting at their 'dresser'.

Some specialised curricula emphasise the teaching of skills that will be needed in adult life from the earliest moments in education. This makes sense where the skills are also of current relevance (sorting cutlery instead of pink bunnies and Christmas trees, for example) but there is a danger that we might limit children's horizons in this way. We would be unhappy to see the training of particular work skills needed in particular occupations (usually of a socially undervalued kind) from an early age, on the assumption that it is the priority to give them access to employment, no matter how menial or below their potential. This may be the function of work skills programmes but it is not educational in the true sense and does nothing to develop that individual's possibilities for more meaningful employment.

AN AGE-APPROPRIATE CURRICULUM

As to the notion of 'age-appropriateness', for most pupils with autism it would be more meaningful to talk of 'person-appropriateness', which takes account of both age and developmental level. Certainly we need to bear in mind that a particular pupil is 17 years old, regardless of his or her developmental level, but equally we should remember the stage of development, regardless of age. And, in autism, that notion of development needs to be further analysed. An individual might be capable of high levels of functioning in terms of, for example, reading and remembering bus timetables for whole districts, but be unable to make a simple bus journey across the town because they cannot sit next to others.

And again, the relevance of sex education clearly changes over the time of an individual's schooling, but that change relates to social and emotional development, not merely to physical development with age. Of course, we are not saying that all teaching should wait for the pupil to achieve the appropriate developmental level. Without positive intervention to teach the developmental levels, most pupils with autism would make little progress. There may also be some aspects of education that need to be taught even though the individual is not developmentally 'ready' for them. Adolescents will need to be prepared for the changes of puberty whether or not they can understand their significance, and they will need sufficient sex instruction to keep them safe and to maintain health and propriety. But it may be confusing and cruel to introduce them to sexually explicit instruction involving emotional states they cannot begin to appreciate, just because they are of an appropriate age.

SKILL ACQUISITION

The rhetoric of the National Curriculum is about knowledge, experience and understanding but it actually stresses skill acquisition in its statements of attainment. Within the broad field of special education, also, the teaching of skills has come to be synonymous with 'education' as opposed to 'care'. Skill acquisition is a by-product of most of the special curriculum packages that pre-dated the National Curriculum and still features in the teaching approach of many special schools. There is a danger, then, that teachers of pupils with autism will end up emphasising skills for particular children even where this is clearly inappropriate. As we have seen, it is difficult to become truly skilful in social or communicative areas without understanding, and too many 'skills' are in fact mere rote habits. Education has to be about more than skill acquisition; it needs to include teaching for increased understanding and should involve care and concern for the quality of the life of the individual with autism.

APPROPRIATENESS OF ENTITLEMENT

Teachers of children with autism are obliged, in most settings, to provide access to the National Curriculum, regardless of any analysis of the appropriateness of that curriculum in meeting the real needs of the children. To accommodate this, working parties have devised ways in which these pupils can be involved in the National Curriculum and one of the authors has edited these access documents.[14] Yet the starting point for this is a curriculum that was not devised with the needs of these pupils (or any other pupils with special needs, in the first instance) in mind; it is not an inclusive curriculum and so it cannot really be the base of inclusive schooling. The move towards giving all pupils the same educational experiences should take account of pupils' ability to respond to, and profit from, those experiences.

Certainly children with autism *are* entitled to be educated, but that means little if we interpret it as entitlement to what passes for education for the majority of people. They are entitled to education according to their own needs and the circumstances of their lives; talk of integration and equality does not alter the fact that the needs of those with autism *are* exceptional and demand exceptional measures if they are to be met. In short, there is a danger that the needs of some pupils with autism may be obscured by the needs of the general; indeed, they may be exposed to a curriculum which is antithetical to their own needs. What is appropriate for the majority of pupils may simply not be appropriate for them.

FROM ENTITLEMENT TO INCLUSION

Education has become increasingly justified and valued not for itself but only as a preparation for life. The assumption is that future quality of life will be ensured by the acquisition of 'useful' skills and knowledge. Apart from the consequent neglect of the educational process, and therefore the quality of that process itself, this assumes that quality of life is a commonly defined concept that is the same for everybody. Educationists, naturally enough, tend to interpret the 'quality of life' from the perspective of the non-autistic without considering what that notion of 'quality' really means for the individual concerned. We cannot know what counts as quality for some of our pupils with autism, but a minimum assumption would surely be that they should be physically and psychologically as comfortable as possible, experience love and care, and benefit from sensitive advocacy. For many, with additional learning difficulties, if they can be helped to develop appropriate and usable ways of expressing their needs, and some way of making and indicating choices, then those would seem to be reasonable educational aims. For pupils with autism their future quality of life is more likely to depend on the degree to which they can learn to live with and understand others than solely on any academic skills they may possess.

'A curriculum for all' would be appropriate if all individuals could benefit from that curriculum. In the context of autism, the slogan needs modifying to 'curriculum *principles* for all'. Such principles would include the notion that priority should always be given to care and concern for the current quality of life of the individual with autism as well as for their future prospects. Individuals have the right to have their interests recognised and respected by the curriculum, which cannot therefore rest solely on predetermined and common experiences and goals. We need, then, to move from current notions of entitlement to a *pre-determined* curriculum, to a notion of 'inclusion' in a curriculum. All pupils, including those with autism, need to be included in a curriculum at the planning stage and not just as modifications to it. Inclusion in education as a human right leads to the notion of common principles that we have raised above, and it means that location and provision become matters of equal opportunity.

AUTISTIC THINKING: IMPLICATIONS FOR PEDAGOGY

EFFECTIVE EDUCATION

We have set out in earlier chapters our notion of the nature of autistic thinking, and we have described the kinds of learning difficulty that arise as a direct result of this particular style. Here we return full circle to the notion because we believe that the way to effective education of those with autism lies in understanding that kind of thinking as well as we are able within the current state of knowledge. In particular, we have stressed throughout this book our belief that teaching should be more than simply a way of modifying behaviour so that it is acceptable, and of increasing the knowledge and skill of the individual as far as possible within the limits of the autistic learning frame. There needs to be an element within the curriculum that seeks to improve the effectiveness of the individual's thinking and learning.

PEDAGOGICAL PRINCIPLES

An unfortunate belief has emerged in the UK of late which suggests that teachers can be trained successfully to deliver predetermined educational programmes, by simply observing 'good practice'. All that is required of them, within this conception, is an ability to carry out instructions, monitor progress towards predetermined goals and finally assess 'results'. In our view this kind of approach is wholly unsuited to the education of any child but it has particular dangers for those with autism. Any effective teaching of such children is going to require a continuous diagnostic monitoring of the process of their thinking and learning. It is simply not enough to judge by outward behaviour, when the template for our understanding of why people do what they do is likely, in the case of autism, to grossly mislead.

There are, in our view, no predetermined steps that the teacher can take that will resolve the problems of educating the child with autism, because such individuals are so different and because they may be different within themselves over time and across situations. Therefore what teachers need are guiding principles which they can apply according to their own judgement within particular situations in the classroom. They need to be informed by their knowledge of autism and of the individual child, and by their own self-knowledge of their capabilities and potential. But the practice of teaching is a matter of balancing pros and cons and making intuitive judgements about the best way to proceed. We would argue that autism presents a particular challenge in that it requires teachers to re-examine their intuitions and to rethink some of their beliefs and attitudes; but they can only do this if they are free of constraining, predetermined, 'necessary' ways of proceeding.

USING AN EXPERIENCING SELF

If we are right in our analysis of a key difficulty in information processing in autism being a failure to develop and utilise an experiencing self, then this may lie within the domains that we label in an earlier chapter as 'unteachable' in principle. In the effort to establish autism as a cognitive developmental disorder rather than an emotional illness, psychologists and teachers have also moved away from teaching and therapeutic approaches that deal with the establishment of 'the self'. It is true that psychodynamic approaches have not been found to be effective in autism (and we are not advocating them), but it also seems that skills-based approaches never get beyond skill acquisition and fail to develop any generalisable ability to learn to learn. It may not be possible to teach individuals with autism to perceive and experience the world in certain ways if they are not biologically predetermined so to do (and it may not be ethically appropriate to try). However, we have suggested that it might be possible to achieve the same (or similar) ends by different routes and we might be able to improve the thinking of individuals with autism by getting them to think 'as if' they had this experiencing self. Indeed many of the more able individuals with autism appear to function as if this were precisely what has occurred. For example, our attempts to use instant photographs of the learner with autism to try to establish autobiographical event memory may enable an 'outside' sense of the self to develop and this may help with problem solving, without necessarily altering the way that events are experienced.

If we are to teach individuals with autism how to learn then we need to move on from a compensatory curriculum operating at a behavioural level. Yet a truly remedial curriculum may not be possible either. What is needed, then, is a compensatory curriculum operating at the cognitive level which aims to give pupils with autism access to cognitive skills that, though not replicating the biologically determined 'natural' ones, can be employed behaviourally 'as if' they do. When working with those with autism then, teachers need to continually draw pupils' attention back to their own role in any problem-solving situation. Pupils need to be helped to work at the level of recognising their own involvement because without such recognition subsequent development of usable memories will not occur.

USING EMOTION

It is common practice in the teaching of all children, and particularly perhaps with those with autism, to look for ways of defusing emotional concomitants of failure or frustration in problem-solving tasks. But in psychological terms we know that real improvements in thinking may only come about if we encourage awareness of the emotional state instead. The dilemma for the teacher, therefore, is how to teach by using emotions and at the same time to manage the emotional context of the classroom. Again, judgements on this can only be made by individual teachers in specific situations. All we can do here is set out what seems to us to be a reasonable principle and leave teachers to act upon it or not as they see fit. The principle must be, then, that those working with autism need to try to establish in the pupil a reflective awareness of his/her own emotional states and this may need to be done in a situation which is 'emotionally charged'.

Certainly, the teacher may need to contain emotional expression in a particular situation but may also need to use it at a reflective level, as discussed in the chapter on emotion. To defuse may be desirable but to defuse and then ignore is less likely to be so, and is not perhaps necessary in terms of classroom 'control'. In our view there are occasions (and the choosing of those occasions is a matter of teacher skill and judgement) where the teacher needs to deliberately try to use the emotion generated within a situation to establish an understanding in the pupil of how he/she felt about the activity; by so doing the aim would be to increase the saliency of the learning for the pupil. In a sense, of course, this puts education within a therapeutic context and in our view this is appropriate when working with autism: education becomes very much a part of a general therapeutic process.

CONCLUSION

We have made the case for critical reflection in the organisation and practice of the education of children with autism. We have also suggested that reflection is both the problem in autistic thinking and the solution, in that children with autism have a difficulty in reflecting which teachers can help them to overcome or circumvent. Understanding children with autism may be intellectually demanding and educating them is most certainly challenging. In our view it is not possible to do the latter effectively without first undertaking the former.

Postscript

It came as something of a surprise to us when writing this book that our problem was not so much what to put in as what to leave out. Our original intention had been to write an all-encompassing book on education and autism but it became clear that this was not possible within the space available. Our solution is apparent in the text; we chose to trace our own notion of how best to educate those with autism from its origins in a particular psychological perspective to a specific way of teaching. There are important issues therefore that we have not tackled, but then perhaps there always are.

One reviewer of our initial book proposal suggested that we should concentrate on practical issues and forget about the 'understanding' bit, saying that this was covered in other texts. We rejected that notion because in the first place our understanding of autism is not available in other texts but, more importantly, because we think it is not possible to educate, in the full sense, without understanding. Our hope is that the reader, having read this far, will now endorse that view. We do not claim to understand autism completely or to have reached any final definitive view of its nature, but we believe that it is only in that striving to understand that a true educational stance can be achieved.

References

1 American Psychiatric Association (1994) *Diagnostic and Statistical Manual of Mental Disorders*, 4th edn (DSM–IV). Washington, DC, American Psychiatric Association.

2 Baron-Cohen, S., Leslie, A. M. & Frith, U. (1985) Does the autistic child have a 'theory of mind'? *Cognition*, **21**, 37–46.

3 Courchesne, E., Saitoh, O., Townsend, J. P. & Yeung-Courchesne, R. (1994) Cerebellar hypoplasia and hyperplasia in infantile autism. *Lancet*, **343**, 1 January, 63–64.

4 DeMyer, M. & DeMyer, K. (1979) *Parents and Children in Autism*. Washington, DC, Winston & Sons.

5 Department of Education and Science (1970) *The Education (Handicapped Children) Act*. London, DES.

6 Department of Education and Science (1978) *Special Educational Needs: Report of the Committee of Enquiry into the Education of Handicapped Children and Young People (Warnock Report)*. London, DES.

7 Dewart, H. & Summers, S. (1988) *The Pragmatics Profile of Early Communication Skills*. Windsor, NFER/Nelson.

8 Doll, E. A. (1965) *Vineland Social Maturity Scale*. Windsor, NFER/Nelson.

9 Frith, U. (1989) *Autism: Explaining the Enigma*. Oxford, Blackwell.

10 Grandin, T. & Scariano, M. (1986) *Emergence, Labelled Autistic*. London, Costello.

11 Hobson, R. P. (1993) *Autism and the Development of Mind*. London, Erlbaum.

12 Jordan, R. R. (1989) An experimental comparison of the understanding and use of speaker–addressee personal pronouns in autistic children. *British Journal of Disorders of Communication*, **24**, 169–179.

13 Jordan, R. R. (1990) *The Option Approach to Autism: Observer Project Report*. London, National Autistic Society.

14 Jordan, R. R. (1991) *The National Curriculum: Access for Pupils with Autism*. London, Inge Wakehurst Trust.

15 Jordan, R. R. (1993) The nature of the linguistic and communication difficulties of children with autism. In D. J. Messer & G. J. Turner (eds), *Critical Influences on Child Language Acquisition and Development*. London, Macmillan.

16 Jordan, R. R. and Powell, S. D. (1990) Improving thinking in autistic children using computer presented activities *Communication*, **24**, 1, 23–25.

17 Kanner, L. (1943) Autistic disturbances of affective contact. *Nervous Child*, **2**, 217–250.

18 Kiernan, C. C. & Reid, B. (1977) *The Pre-Verbal Communication Schedule*. Windsor, NFER/Nelson.

19 Kiernan, C. C., Reid, B. & Goldbart, J. (1987) *Focus on Language and Communication*. Manchester, Manchester University Press.

20 Mesibov, G. B. & Landrus, R. I. *Structured Teaching*. North Carolina, Workshop Publications.

21 National Autistic Society (1993) *Approaches to Autism*, 2nd edn. London,

National Autistic Society.

22 National Curriculum Council (1989) *Curriculum Guidance 2: A Curriculum for All*. York, National Curriculum Council.

23 Nind, M. & Hewett, D. (1988) Interaction as curriculum. *British Journal of Special Education*, 15, 55–57.

24 Oshima-Takane, Y. & Benaroya, S. (1989) An alternative view of pronominal errors in autistic children. *Journal of Autism and Developmental Disorders*, 19, 73–85.

25 Powell, S. D. & Jordan, R. R. (1993) Being subjective about autistic thinking and learning to learn. *Educational Psychology*, 13, 3–4, 359–370.

26 Riding, R. J. & Powell, S. D. (1989) *Learn to Think*. Birmingham, Learning and Training Technology.

27 Ripich, D. N. & Spinelli, F. M. (1985) An ethnographic approach to assessment and intervention. In D. N. Ripich & F. M. Spinelli, *School Discourse Problems*. London, Taylor & Francis.

28 Sacks, O. (1993) A neurologist's notebook: an anthropologist on Mars. *The New Yorker*, 27 December, pp. 106–125.

29 Schopler, E. and Mesibov, G. B. (eds) (1988) *Diagnosis and Assessment in Autism*. New York, Plenum Press.

30 Segal, S. S. (1965) *No Child is Ineducable: Special Education Provision and Trends*. Oxford, Pergamon.

31 Watson, L. R. (1985) The TEACCH communication curriculum. In E. Schopler & G. Mesibov (eds), *Communication Problems in Autism*. New York, Plenum Press.

32 Watson, L., Lord, C., Schaffer, B. & Schopler, E. (1989) *Teaching Spontaneous Communication to Autistic and Developmentally Handicapped Children*. New York, Irvington.

33 Williams, D. (1992) *Nobody Nowhere*. London, Doubleday.

34 Wing, L. (1988) The continuum of autistic characteristics. In E. Schopler & G. Mesibov (eds), *Diagnosis and Assessment in Autism*. New York, Plenum Press.

35 Wing, L. & Gould, J. (1979) Severe impairments of social interaction and associated abnormalities in children: epidemiology and classification. *Journal of Autism and Developmental Disorders*, 9, 11–29.

36 World Health Organisation (1990) *Mental Disorders: a Glossary and Guide to their Classification in Accordance with the 10th Revision of the International Classification of Diseases (ICD–10)*. Geneva, World Health Organisation.

Index

Numbers in **bold** refer to main sections

Related titles of interest...

The Development of Communication
From Social Interaction to Language
David J. Messer

Provides an authoritative review of the development of communication from birth to three years. The book will be important reading for second-and third-year undergraduates in linguistics and cognitive science.

0-471-94076-3   352pp   1994   Hardback
0-471 94421-1   352pp   1995   Paperback

Handbook of Spelling
Theory, Process and Intervention
Edited by **Gordon D.A. Brown** and **Nick C. Ellis**
Foreword by **Uta Frith**

With the increasing demand for information about spelling performance, this book is a timely addition to the current literature. It adopts the multidisciplinary methods of cognitive science to cover key issues including writing systems; information-processing models; representation; computational models; connectionist approaches; analyses of errors; and spelling instruction and remediation.

0-471-94342-8   546pp   1994   Hardback

Treatment of Autistic Children
Patricia Howlin and **Michael Rutter**

"This book will no doubt become a must for professionals working with autistic children as well as for those involved in clinical research. I found the book quite stimulating."

BEHAVIOUR RESEARCH AND THERAPY

0-471-92638-8   310pp   1989   Paperback

DYSLEXIA
An International Journal of Research and Practice
The Journal of the British Dyslexia Association

Editor: **T.R. Miles,** Dyslexia Unit, University of Wales, Bangor, UK
ISSN: 1076-9242